Discovering Vegan Spain: A Culinary and Cultural Expedition with Delectable Vegan Recipes Across Spain

"Embark on a sensory journey through the heart of Spain with 'Discovering Vegan Spain.' This gastronomic odyssey isn't just a collection of recipes; it's an invitation to savor the richness of plant-based delights in each region, unearthing the cultural tapestry that binds veganism with the vibrant soul of Spanish cuisine. This book is your compass to navigating the delectable fusion of tradition and innovation, proving that a vegan lifestyle in Spain is not just a choice but a celebration of flavor, diversity, and mindful living."

Rami Georgiev

Dedicated to the bold souls with a plant-powered palate and a wanderlust for Spain. To those who believe that the journey to a compassionate lifestyle is also an exploration of diverse flavors, cultures, and traditions. May this book be your compass, guiding you through the vegan tapestry of Spain, where each recipe and insight is dedicated to your culinary and cultural adventure. Here's to the dreamers, the seekers, and the compassionate hearts who find joy in every vegan discovery on Spanish soil.

Introduction:

Welcome to a culinary odyssey that transcends the boundaries of tradition and embraces the vibrant tapestry of plant-based living in the heart of Spain. "Discovering Vegan Spain" is an exploration designed for the intrepid souls whose love for veganism intertwines seamlessly with their passion for travel. In these pages, we embark on a journey that extends beyond recipes; it's an immersive experience into the diverse landscapes, rich cultures, and tantalizing flavors that define the vegan tapestry of each Spanish region.

Spanning from the bustling streets of Madrid to the sun-kissed shores of Barcelona, the historic charm of Seville, the culinary wonders of Valencia, and the enchanting alleys of Granada, this book serves as your compass, guiding you through a gastronomic expedition that celebrates plant-based delights against the backdrop of Spain's cultural kaleidoscope.

Here, veganism is not merely a dietary choice; it is a celebration of the artistry that arises when compassionate living meets the warmth of Spanish hospitality. As you turn each page, prepare to uncover the secrets of veganized classics, indulge in regional specialties, and experience the joy of savoring authentic flavors without compromising ethical values.

"Discovering Vegan Spain" is an invitation to the curious wanderers, the culinary enthusiasts, and the conscious explorers who seek to unravel the magic that unfolds when a plant-based lifestyle encounters the soul-stirring allure of Spain. Whether you are a seasoned vegan traveler or a newcomer to the world of plant-based living, this book is crafted to be your trusted companion on a journey where every recipe tells a story, and every chapter is an invitation to savor the essence of Spain through the lens of compassionate and mindful choices.

Buckle up for a sensory voyage where tradition meets innovation, and every dish is a testament to the boundless creativity that flourishes in the fusion of veganism and Spanish culinary heritage. ¡Buen provecho and happy exploring!

Welcome to Vegan Spain

In the heart of Spain, where centuries-old traditions intertwine with the rhythm of modern life, a vibrant and compassionate culinary revolution has taken root. Welcome to the land where the sizzle of olive oil meets the fragrance of saffron, and where veganism, like an eager vine, has woven its way into the very fabric of Spanish gastronomy.

The Tapestry of Veganism:

Spain, known for its historic cities, sun-soaked landscapes, and a culinary heritage that spans regions, welcomes the conscious traveler and the plant-powered connoisseur alike. As you step onto the cobbled streets of Madrid, breathe in the ocean breeze in Barcelona, or wander through the orange-scented gardens of Seville, know that you are about to embark on a sensory journey like no other.

Tradition Meets Innovation:

"Discovering Vegan Spain" is an invitation to explore the marriage of tradition and innovation, where the reverence for local ingredients collides harmoniously with the artistry of vegan culinary expression. Here, the rustic charm of centuries-old recipes meets the ingenuity of plant-based adaptations, creating a symphony of flavors that echoes through bustling markets and quaint eateries alike.

Gastronomic Haven of Madrid:

Madrid, with its bustling streets and lively plazas, emerges as a vegan gastronomic haven. Picture yourself savoring the crispy perfection of vegan churros, indulging in a bowl of plant-based Cocido Madrileño, and relishing the vibrant colors of veganized Pisto Manchego. Each dish, a nod to tradition, each bite, an ode to compassionate living.

Barcelona's Coastal Elegance:

As we journey eastward to Barcelona, the city's coastal elegance unfolds in a tapestry of plant-based delights. Vegan paella, infused with the essence of saffron, graces the tables, while Escudella i Carn d'Olla finds its plant-based counterpart. A glass of vegan Cava Sangria in hand, you find yourself immersed in the dynamic dance of innovation and cultural reverence.

Seville's Timeless Charm:

Seville, with its timeless charm, invites you to explore traditional flavors with a vegan twist. Salmorejo, transformed with vegan Jamón, and Espárragos de Navarra served with almond-based sauces, transport you to the heart of Andalusian culinary heritage. The air is infused with the aroma of Gazpacho Andaluz, a refreshing elixir of tomatoes, peppers, and garlic.

Valencia's Culinary Adventures:

Valencia, a haven for culinary adventurers, unfolds its treasures with vegan paella Valenciana, a masterpiece of saffron-infused rice and fresh vegetables. All i Pebre, the Valencian eel stew, finds a vegan rendition, and

Fideuà Marinera introduces you to the tantalizing world of vegan seafood. Valencia's culinary adventures are an invitation to savor the diversity of plant-based living.

Granada's Tapestry of Vegan Tapas:

As we reach Granada, the city's historic allure mingles with the enchantment of vegan tapas. Papas a lo Pobre, Zanahorias Aliñadas, and Remojón Granadino Salad showcase the artistry of veganized traditional dishes. Conclude your culinary journey with Tinto de Verano Sorbet, a frozen ode to Granada's iconic drink.

An Invitation to Explore:

"Discovering Vegan Spain" is not just a cookbook; it is an invitation to explore the uncharted territories where veganism and Spanish cuisine intertwine. With each recipe, immerse yourself in the stories, the flavors, and the cultural nuances that make Spain a tapestry of vegan delights. Whether you are a seasoned vegan traveler or a newcomer to the world of plant-based living, this chapter beckons you to savor the essence of Spain through the lens of compassionate and mindful choices.

Here's to the Dreamers, the Seekers, and the Compassionate Hearts:

May your journey through "Discovering Vegan Spain" be a celebration of flavor, diversity, and mindful living. As you turn the pages, may you find inspiration in every recipe and may each dish be a testament to the boundless creativity that flourishes in the fusion of veganism and Spanish culinary heritage. ¡Buen provecho and happy exploring!

A Brief Overview of Veganism in Spain

In the tapestry of Spain's culinary heritage, the threads of veganism weave a narrative of change, consciousness, and a growing awareness of the impact of our choices on the planet and its inhabitants. As we delve into the cultural nuances and historical shifts that have shaped the landscape of veganism in Spain, we find a story as diverse and rich as the regions themselves.

Historical Perspectives:

To understand veganism in Spain is to trace its roots through time. While traditional Spanish cuisine has long been celebrated for its robust flavors, centered around meats and dairy, the tides have shifted. The journey of plant-based living in Spain begins with a subtle rebellion against culinary norms, an exploration of alternative ingredients, and an ever-growing community of individuals seeking a more compassionate way of life.

Cultural Influences on Vegan Cuisine:

Veganism in Spain is not merely a dietary choice; it's a cultural evolution. Influences from Mediterranean traditions, with their abundance of fresh fruits, vegetables, and olive oil, lay a foundation for plant-based exploration. The diversity of Spain's regions brings forth a myriad of locally sourced ingredients, transforming traditional dishes into vibrant, vegan interpretations that honor both heritage and sustainability.

Vegan Advocacy and Awareness:

Over the years, vegan advocacy has found its voice in Spain. From grassroots movements to the rise of social media influencers, the conversation around plant-based living has gained momentum. Restaurants proudly feature vegan options on their menus, and cities embrace the trend with vegan festivals, markets, and a growing number of cruelty-free establishments. The cultural shift towards a more plant-centric lifestyle is palpable, reflecting a collective consciousness toward mindful and ethical choices.

Plant-Powered Influencers and Chefs:

The emergence of vegan influencers and chefs has played a pivotal role in reshaping Spain's culinary landscape. From sharing delectable plant-based recipes to promoting the environmental and ethical benefits of vegan living, these individuals have become catalysts for change. Their innovative approaches to veganizing traditional dishes inspire a new generation to embrace compassionate eating without compromising on taste.

Veganism Beyond the Plate:

Veganism in Spain extends beyond culinary preferences; it permeates various aspects of lifestyle. From cruelty-free fashion to eco-conscious living, the ethos of veganism intertwines with the broader spectrum of ethical choices. Animal sanctuaries, eco-friendly practices, and a growing awareness of the environmental impact of food choices contribute to a holistic understanding of veganism that transcends the dinner table.

Looking Forward:

As we navigate the landscapes of veganism in Spain, it becomes evident that the movement is not a fleeting trend but a transformative force. The future holds the promise of more plant-powered innovations, a deeper integration of ethical choices into mainstream living, and a continued celebration of the intersection between tradition and conscious living.

Conclusion:

"A Brief Overview of Veganism in Spain" is an introduction to a journey that goes beyond recipes. It is an acknowledgment of the evolving tapestry of plant-based living in a country deeply rooted in culinary tradition. As we venture into the subsequent chapters, let this overview be a lens through which we perceive the diverse and dynamic landscape of veganism in the beautiful and multifaceted Spain.

Chapter 2: Veganism and Spanish Culture

In the heart of Spain, where centuries of cultural heritage and modern ethical considerations intersect, the dialogue between veganism and Spanish culture unfolds as a dynamic exploration of tradition, innovation, and conscientious living. This chapter delves into the rich tapestry of Spanish culture, examining the intersections where culinary practices, historical values, and the ethos of veganism intertwine.

Historical Perspectives

In the sun-drenched landscapes of Spain, where ancient civilizations left their imprints on culture and cuisine, the historical perspectives of veganism unfold as a nuanced narrative. Beyond the culinary traditions that have defined Spain's past, this chapter delves into the evolution of attitudes towards food, animals, and the emergence of veganism against the backdrop of history.

Prehistoric Foundations:

Long before the sprawling cities and medieval castles, Spain was home to prehistoric communities whose diets were primarily plant-based. As we trace the footprints left by early inhabitants, we uncover a connection between ancient foraging practices and the roots of veganism, offering a glimpse into the deep history of plant-centric sustenance.

Influence of Moorish Culture:

The Moorish occupation of Spain from the 8th to the 15th century left an indelible mark on the country's culinary landscape. With an emphasis on fruits, nuts, and aromatic spices, Moorish influences sowed the seeds for a diverse and plant-centric culinary heritage. Veganism, in its historical context, draws inspiration from the Moorish era's emphasis on plant-based ingredients.

Medieval Gastronomy:

In medieval Spain, culinary traditions blossomed in royal courts and noble households. While meats and dairy were esteemed, historical texts reveal an intricate interplay of flavors that included an array of fruits, vegetables, and grains. This period becomes a tapestry where veganism finds historical echoes, not as a defined movement, but as an undercurrent in the diverse gastronomic spectrum.

Inquisition and Culinary Change:

The Spanish Inquisition marked a tumultuous period in history, impacting every facet of life, including dietary habits. As religious and cultural dynamics shifted, dietary restrictions became a reflection of identity. This chapter explores how this period of upheaval contributed to a reshaping of culinary practices and laid the groundwork for future considerations of ethical eating.

Colonial Influences and New World Ingredients:

Spain's exploration and colonization of the Americas brought a trove of new ingredients to its shores. The exchange of culinary cultures introduced a plethora of fruits, vegetables, and grains that enriched the Spanish pantry. This influx of New World ingredients played a role in diversifying the Spanish diet, offering a broader palette for plant-based exploration.

Industrialization and Changing Diets:

The industrial revolution in the 19th century marked a transformative era, impacting not only the way Spaniards lived but also how they ate. The shift towards urbanization and industrialization brought changes to dietary patterns, with an increasing reliance on processed foods. This chapter examines how these changes set the stage for later discussions on sustainable and ethical eating.

Conclusion:

As we navigate the historical perspectives of veganism in Spain, we uncover a tapestry woven with threads of foraging ancestors, Moorish influences, medieval gastronomy, periods of upheaval, colonial exchanges, and the complexities of industrialization. Each era leaves its mark, contributing to the nuanced story of how Spain's relationship with plant-based living has evolved over time. This historical journey sets the stage for understanding the contemporary dynamics between tradition, innovation, and ethical considerations in the chapters to come.

Cultural Influences on Vegan Cuisine

In the vibrant tapestry of Spain's culinary landscape, where the echoes of history reverberate alongside contemporary trends, the fusion of cultural influences shapes the evolution of vegan cuisine. This chapter embarks on a journey through the diverse regions of Spain, exploring the intricate dance between tradition, innovation, and the ever-expanding realm of plant-based gastronomy.

Medley of Mediterranean Traditions:

At the heart of Spanish culture lies the Mediterranean, a sea whose influence extends far beyond its shores. The sun-drenched fields of olive groves, the abundance of citrus fruits, and the robust flavors of herbs like rosemary and thyme create a medley of Mediterranean traditions. Vegan cuisine in Spain becomes a celebration of these flavors, infusing dishes with the essence of the sun-kissed landscapes.

Regional Varieties:

Spain's culinary map is a mosaic of regional varieties, each offering a unique palette of ingredients and cooking techniques. From the bold spices of Andalusian dishes to the seafood-centric delights of coastal regions, veganism weaves into these regional tapestries, adding a new layer of creativity while respecting the authenticity of each locale.

The Art of Tapas:

Tapas, the small, flavorful dishes that define Spanish social dining, are a cultural institution. In this chapter, we explore how vegan tapas have become an art form, showcasing the diverse flavors and textures that plant-based ingredients can offer. From patatas bravas with vegan aioli to marinated olives and gazpacho shooters, vegan tapas embrace the essence of communal dining.

Celebration of Seasonal Produce:

Cultural influences on vegan cuisine in Spain are intimately tied to the celebration of seasonal produce. As the seasons shift, so do the offerings on the vegan table. From the juicy tomatoes of summer in Andalusia to the earthy root vegetables in the colder months of the north, vegan dishes become a reflection of the cyclical rhythm of nature.

Innovative Takes on Traditional Dishes:

Traditional Spanish dishes, deeply rooted in centuries-old recipes, undergo innovative transformations in the hands of contemporary chefs. This chapter explores how plant-based renditions of classics like paella, cocido, and patatas bravas seamlessly integrate into the culinary narrative, offering a fresh perspective without compromising on the soulful essence of these time-honored creations.

Culinary Fusion in Urban Centers:

In bustling urban centers like Madrid and Barcelona, where diverse influences converge, vegan cuisine becomes a canvas for culinary fusion. The intersections of global flavors, local ingredients, and a growing consciousness around ethical eating create a dynamic culinary landscape where veganism is not just a dietary choice but a vibrant expression of cultural fusion.

Conclusion:

"Cultural Influences on Vegan Cuisine" is a chapter that invites readers to savor the nuances of a culinary renaissance where tradition and innovation coalesce. As we traverse the diverse regions and urban hubs of Spain, let this exploration be a celebration of the dynamic interplay between cultural influences and the ever-evolving canvas of vegan gastronomy. The culinary journey continues, promising a tapestry of flavors that honor the roots of tradition while embracing the boundless possibilities that plant-based living brings to the table.

Chapter 3: Navigating Vegan-Friendly Cities

Step into the enchanting realms of Spain's bustling cities, where the vibrancy of urban life converges with the flourishing tapestry of vegan-friendly options. In this chapter, we embark on a journey through the bustling streets, vibrant markets, and eclectic neighborhoods of Madrid, Barcelona, Seville, Valencia, and Granada—cities where veganism isn't just a dietary choice but a dynamic expression of culinary innovation and compassion.

Madrid: A Vegan Gastronomic Haven:

The Spanish capital, Madrid, unfolds as a vegan gastronomic haven, where traditional flavors harmonize with plant-based ingenuity. Wander through the streets, and discover the sizzle of vegan churros, the heartiness of vegan Cocido Madrileño, and the savory notes of veganized Pisto Manchego. Madrid's vegan scene beckons, inviting you to savor the city's rich culinary heritage with a compassionate twist.

Barcelona: Plant-Based Delights by the Sea:

As we venture to Barcelona, the city by the sea, plant-based delights abound in a symphony of flavors. Indulge in the aromatic vegan paella, explore the textures of vegan Escudella i Carn d'Olla, and bask in the sweetness of vegan Crema Catalana. The culinary journey in Barcelona is a celebration of plant-based gastronomy against the backdrop of the Mediterranean's azure beauty.

Seville: Traditional Flavors with a Vegan Twist:

Seville, with its timeless charm, offers a tapestry of traditional flavors with a vegan twist. Immerse yourself in the cool embrace of vegan Salmorejo, savor the elegance of Espárragos de Navarra in vegan style, and relish the heartiness of vegan Berza Gitana. Seville's vegan offerings are a testament to the city's ability to blend tradition with the innovation of plant-based living.

Valencia: Culinary Adventures in Veganism:

Valencia, known for its culinary adventures, presents a medley of plant-based delights. Taste the richness of vegan Paella Valenciana, experience the depth of flavor in vegan All i Pebre, and journey into the ocean with vegan Fideuà Marinera. Valencia's culinary landscape is an adventure for the palate, where plant-based ingredients shine in the region's vibrant gastronomy.

Granada: Exploring Vegan Tapas:

In Granada, where the echoes of history linger in every corner, vegan tapas take center stage. Delight in the simplicity of vegan Papas a lo Pobre, relish the flavors of vegan Almond Soup, and discover the charm of vegan Zanahorias Aliñadas. Granada's vegan tapas scene invites you to explore the city's culinary heritage through a plant-based lens.

Navigating Vegan-Friendly Urban Centers:

Beyond individual cities, this chapter delves into the art of navigating vegan-friendly urban centers. Discover the array of vegan options in markets, cafes, and restaurants, and learn the nuances of ordering vegan in a country that treasures its culinary traditions. Navigating vegan-friendly cities in Spain becomes an adventure, where every street corner holds the promise of a delectable and compassionate discovery.

Madrid: A Vegan Gastronomic Haven

Nestled in the heart of Spain, Madrid emerges as a vibrant metropolis where the rich tapestry of traditional flavors mingles seamlessly with the innovation of vegan gastronomy. In this chapter, we embark on a sensory journey through the bustling streets and lively plazas of Madrid, exploring the city's diverse and delectable vegan

Vegan Churros:
Our journey begins with the iconic Spanish delight – churros. Madrid's streets come alive with the sizzle of vegan churros, golden and crispy, served with a dusting of sugar. Dip them in luscious chocolate sauce or enjoy them on their own, an indulgence that captures the essence of Spanish street food.

Ingredients:

For the Churro Dough:

1 cup water

1/2 cup vegan margarine

2 tablespoons brown sugar

1/4 teaspoon salt

1 cup all-purpose flour

1/2 cup almond flour (optional, for added flavor)

1 teaspoon vanilla extract

For Frying:

Vegetable oil, for frying

For Coating:

1/2 cup granulated sugar

1 teaspoon ground cinnamon

Instructions:

Prepare the Coating:

In a shallow bowl, mix the granulated sugar and ground cinnamon. Set aside for coating the churros later.

Prepare the Churro Dough:

In a saucepan over medium heat, combine water, vegan margarine, brown sugar, and salt. Bring the mixture to a boil.

Reduce the heat to low and add the all-purpose flour (and almond flour if using) all at once. Stir vigorously with a wooden spoon until the mixture forms a ball. Remove from heat.

Add Vanilla Extract:

Allow the dough to cool for a few minutes, and then stir in the vanilla extract until well combined.

Pipe the Churros:

Heat vegetable oil in a large pan or deep fryer to 350°F (175°C).

Transfer the churro dough to a piping bag fitted with a large star tip.

Pipe 4 to 6 inch strips of dough directly into the hot oil, using scissors or a knife to cut the dough.

Fry the Churros:

Fry the churros until golden brown, turning them occasionally to ensure even cooking. This usually takes about 2-4 minutes per batch.

Coat with Sugar and Cinnamon:

Immediately roll the hot churros in the cinnamon-sugar mixture, ensuring they are well coated.

Serve Warm:

Serve the vegan churros warm with your favorite dipping sauce. Vegan chocolate sauce or fruit coulis are great options.

Enjoy!

Enjoy your delicious vegan churros as a delightful treat or dessert.

These vegan churros are crispy on the outside, soft on the inside, and will surely satisfy your sweet cravings. Feel free to get creative with your dipping sauces or add a sprinkle of powdered sugar for extra sweetness.

Cocido Madrileño - Vegan Style:

Step into the warmth of Madrid's culinary heritage with a vegan twist on Cocido Madrileño. This hearty stew, traditionally laden with meats, transforms into a plant-based marvel featuring chickpeas, vegetables, and savory vegan chorizo. Each spoonful is a journey into the heart of Spanish comfort food.

Ingredients:

For the Stew:

1 cup dried chickpeas, soaked overnight

2 tablespoons olive oil

1 large onion, chopped

3 cloves garlic, minced

2 medium carrots, peeled and chopped

2 medium potatoes, peeled and chopped

1 leek, cleaned and sliced

1 cup green beans, chopped

1 cup cabbage, shredded

2 ripe tomatoes, chopped

1 bay leaf

1 teaspoon paprika

1 teaspoon ground cumin

Salt and pepper to taste

8 cups vegetable broth or water

For the Saffron Rice:

1 cup white rice

A pinch of saffron threads

2 cups vegetable broth

Salt to taste

For Serving:

Chopped fresh parsley

Lemon wedges

Instructions:

Prepare the Chickpeas:

Drain and rinse the soaked chickpeas. In a large pot, cover them with water and bring to a boil. Reduce heat and simmer until chickpeas are tender, about 1 to 1.5 hours. Drain and set aside.

Prepare the Stew:

In a large pot, heat olive oil over medium heat. Add onions and garlic, sauté until softened.

Add carrots, potatoes, leek, green beans, and cabbage to the pot. Stir well.

Add the chopped tomatoes, bay leaf, paprika, cumin, salt, and pepper. Stir to combine.

Pour in the vegetable broth or water. Bring the mixture to a boil, then reduce the heat to low and simmer for about 30 minutes or until the vegetables are tender.

Add the cooked chickpeas to the pot and simmer for an additional 15-20 minutes to allow the flavors to meld. Adjust seasoning if needed.

Prepare the Saffron Rice:

In a separate pot, combine rice, saffron threads, vegetable broth, and salt. Bring to a boil, then reduce the heat to low, cover, and simmer until the rice is cooked and the liquid is absorbed.

Serve:

Serve the vegan Cocido Madrileño hot, with a spoonful of saffron rice in each bowl.

Garnish with chopped fresh parsley and provide lemon wedges on the side.

Enjoy your vegan twist on this classic Spanish stew!

This vegan Cocido Madrileño captures the rich flavors of the traditional dish while omitting the meat. It's a hearty and comforting stew that's perfect for colder days.

Vegan Pisto Manchego

Next on our gastronomic tour is Pisto Manchego, a rustic Spanish ratatouille bursting with the flavors of sun-ripened vegetables. Madrid's veganized Pisto Manchego is a celebration of local produce, showcasing the region's commitment to culinary authenticity while embracing the diversity of plant-based living.

Ingredients:

2 tablespoons olive oil

1 large onion, finely chopped

2 cloves garlic, minced

2 bell peppers (red and green), diced

2 medium zucchinis, diced

1 large eggplant, diced

4 ripe tomatoes, peeled, seeded, and chopped (or 1 can of diced tomatoes)

1 teaspoon smoked paprika

1/2 teaspoon sweet paprika

Salt and pepper to taste

Fresh parsley, chopped, for garnish

Instructions:

Prepare the Vegetables:

Peel and seed the tomatoes. To peel them, score a small "X" at the bottom, blanch in boiling water for 30 seconds, then transfer to an ice bath. The skin should easily peel off.

Dice all the vegetables into evenly sized pieces.

Cook the Pisto:

In a large skillet or pan, heat olive oil over medium heat.

Add the chopped onion and garlic, sautéing until softened and translucent.

Add Vegetables:

Add the diced bell peppers, zucchini, and eggplant to the pan. Stir well to combine.

Seasoning:

Add the chopped tomatoes, smoked paprika, sweet paprika, salt, and pepper. Stir to combine all the ingredients.

Simmer:

Reduce the heat to low, cover the pan, and let the mixture simmer for about 25-30 minutes, or until the vegetables are tender.

Adjust Seasoning:

Taste and adjust the seasoning as needed. You can add more salt, pepper, or paprika according to your preference.

Garnish and Serve:

Garnish the Vegan Pisto Manchego with freshly chopped parsley before serving.

Serve Warm:

Serve the vegan pisto warm as a main dish or a side. It's delicious on its own or accompanied by crusty bread or rice.

Optional Additions:

Feel free to customize your Vegan Pisto Manchego by adding other vegetables like mushrooms or green beans.

Enjoy your Vegan Pisto Manchego, a flavorful and colorful Spanish dish that's both healthy and satisfying!

Vegan Patatas a la Brava with Aioli

Indulge in the zesty flavors of vegan Patatas a la Brava, Madrid's beloved crispy potatoes drizzled with a spicy tomato sauce. Accompanied by a rich and garlicky vegan aioli, this dish exemplifies the fusion of traditional tapas with the contemporary creativity of the city's vegan culinary scene.

Ingredients:

For the Patatas:

4 medium-sized potatoes, peeled and cut into small cubes

3 tablespoons olive oil

Salt to taste

For the Brava Sauce:

1 tablespoon olive oil

1 small onion, finely chopped

2 cloves garlic, minced

1 teaspoon smoked paprika

1/2 teaspoon sweet paprika

1/4 teaspoon cayenne pepper (adjust to taste for spice)

1 can (14 oz) crushed tomatoes

Salt and pepper to taste

1 tablespoon red wine vinegar

For the Vegan Aioli:

1/2 cup vegan mayonnaise

1 clove garlic, minced

1 tablespoon lemon juice

Salt to taste

Instructions:

For the Patatas:

Preheat the oven to 425°F (220°C).

Toss the potato cubes with olive oil and a pinch of salt.

Spread the potatoes on a baking sheet in a single layer.

Bake for 25-30 minutes or until the potatoes are golden brown and crispy, flipping them halfway through.

For the Brava Sauce:

In a saucepan, heat olive oil over medium heat.

Add chopped onions and cook until they become translucent.

Add minced garlic and cook for an additional minute.

Stir in the smoked paprika, sweet paprika, and cayenne pepper.

Pour in the crushed tomatoes, season with salt and pepper, and simmer for 15-20 minutes.

Add red wine vinegar, adjust seasoning, and set the sauce aside.

For the Vegan Aioli:

In a small bowl, whisk together vegan mayonnaise, minced garlic, lemon juice, and salt. Adjust the flavors to your liking.

Assemble:

Place the crispy potatoes on a serving dish.

Spoon the Brava sauce generously over the potatoes.

Drizzle the vegan aioli on top.

Serve:

Garnish with chopped fresh parsley if desired.

Serve the Vegan Patatas a la Brava with Aioli immediately as a delightful tapas dish or side.

Enjoy the bold flavors of the crispy potatoes, spicy tomato sauce, and creamy aioli in this vegan twist on a classic Spanish tapas favorite!

Madrid's Vegan Tapas Scene

As the sun sets over Madrid, immerse yourself in the vivacity of the city's vegan tapas scene. From marinated olives to Gazpacho shooters, each bite tells a story of communal dining and the social fabric that defines Spanish culture. Madrid's vegan tapas offerings invite you to savor the variety and conviviality of shared plates.

Gazpacho Shots:

Serve small shot glasses of traditional Spanish gazpacho, a refreshing cold soup made with tomatoes, peppers, cucumbers, and onions. Garnish with a drizzle of olive oil and fresh herbs.

Pan con Tomate (Tomato Bread):

Toasted bread rubbed with garlic and ripe tomatoes, drizzled with olive oil, and sprinkled with sea salt. It's a simple and classic tapa.

Patatas Bravas:

Roasted or fried potatoes served with a spicy tomato sauce (brava sauce) and a vegan aioli. Ensure the potatoes are crispy on the outside and tender on the inside.

Champiñones al Ajillo (Garlic Mushrooms):

Sautéed mushrooms with garlic, olive oil, and parsley. Add a splash of white wine for extra flavor.

Aceitunas Marinadas (Marinated Olives):

A mix of marinated olives with garlic, herbs, and citrus zest. Serve them in small bowls as a refreshing palate cleanser.

Pimientos de Padrón:

Blistered Padrón peppers seasoned with sea salt. Most are mild, but the occasional one may surprise with some heat.

Espárragos Trigueros (Grilled Asparagus):

Grilled asparagus spears seasoned with olive oil, sea salt, and a squeeze of lemon.

Tostas de Aguacate (Avocado Toasts):

Crusty bread topped with mashed avocado, cherry tomatoes, red onion, and a sprinkle of smoked paprika.

Hummus con Pimientos Asados (Hummus with Roasted Peppers):

Creamy hummus served with strips of roasted red and yellow peppers. Drizzle with olive oil and sprinkle with cumin.

Albóndigas de Lentejas (Lentil Meatballs):

Lentil-based meatballs seasoned with Spanish spices and served with a rich tomato sauce.

Berengenas Rellenas de Ajo Blanco (Stuffed Eggplants with Ajo Blanco):

Eggplant halves filled with a traditional Spanish ajo blanco sauce made with almonds, garlic, bread, and olive oil.

Vegan Spanish Tortilla Bites:

Miniature versions of the classic Spanish tortilla made with potatoes and onions. Serve them in bite-sized portions.

Conclusion:

Madrid, with its bustling energy and a rich culinary tapestry, emerges as a vegan gastronomic haven. In this chapter, we've explored the city's iconic treats, transformed traditional dishes into plant-based delights, and reveled in the lively ambiance of vegan tapas culture. As you turn the page, may the essence of Madrid's vegan offerings linger, inviting you to savor the diversity and innovation that define this captivating city's plant-powered cuisine. ¡Buen provecho!

As we journey to the captivating shores of Barcelona, a city infused with the briny essence of the Mediterranean, we dive into a chapter that unfolds the plant-based treasures found in this coastal paradise. From the iconic paella to the sweet finale of Crema Catalana, Barcelona invites us to savor a symphony of flavors that celebrates both tradition and the vibrant innovation of vegan gastronomy.

Vegan Paella

Barcelona, with its proximity to the sea, beckons us with the fragrant allure of vegan paella. Infused with saffron, this iconic dish transforms into a masterpiece of plant-based flavors. Each grain of rice, every succulent vegetable, and the depth of saffron-infused broth create a melody that captures the essence of Barcelona's culinary spirit.

Ingredients:

For the Sofrito:

2 tablespoons olive oil

1 onion, finely chopped

2 bell peppers (preferably red and green), diced

3 cloves garlic, minced

1 large tomato, diced

1 teaspoon smoked paprika

1/2 teaspoon saffron threads (optional, for color and flavor)

Salt and pepper to taste

For the Paella:

2 cups paella rice (or short-grain rice)

1/2 cup dry white wine (optional)

4 cups vegetable broth

1 cup artichoke hearts, quartered

1 cup cherry tomatoes, halved

1 cup green beans, trimmed and cut into bite-sized pieces

1 cup peas (fresh or frozen)

Lemon wedges for serving

Fresh parsley, chopped, for garnish

Instructions:

1. Prepare the Sofrito:

In a large paella pan or a wide, shallow skillet, heat olive oil over medium heat.

Add chopped onions and bell peppers. Sauté until softened.

Add minced garlic and cook for an additional minute until fragrant.

Stir in diced tomatoes, smoked paprika, saffron threads (if using), salt, and pepper. Cook for another 5 minutes until the tomatoes break down and the mixture becomes a sofrito.

2. Add the Rice and Wine:

Add the paella rice to the sofrito, stirring to coat the rice with the flavors.

Pour in the white wine (if using) and let it cook for a couple of minutes until the alcohol evaporates.

3. Cooking the Paella:

Add vegetable broth to the pan and bring the mixture to a simmer.

Arrange artichoke hearts, cherry tomatoes, green beans, and peas evenly across the pan.

Reduce the heat to low and let the paella simmer gently. Avoid stirring too much; paella forms a delicious crust, called "socarrat," at the bottom.

Cook until the rice is tender and has absorbed the liquid, about 20-25 minutes. Add more broth if needed.

4. Serve:

Once the rice is cooked, remove the paella from heat and let it rest for a few minutes.

Garnish with chopped fresh parsley and serve with lemon wedges on the side.

Serve directly from the paella pan, allowing everyone to enjoy the socarrat.

5. Enjoy:

Enjoy your Vegan Paella as a flavorful and satisfying one-pan dish!

This vegan version of paella captures the essence of the traditional Spanish dish, offering a delicious and plant-based twist. Serve it with a side salad or some crusty bread for a complete and satisfying meal. ¡Buen provecho!

Vegan Escudella i Carn d'Olla

Explore the heartiness of Barcelona's winter traditions with a vegan twist on Escudella i Carn d'Olla. This traditional Catalan dish, usually meat-laden, becomes a celebration of pulses, vegetables, and hearty vegan alternatives. As you savor the robust flavors, Barcelona's commitment to culinary innovation shines through.

Ingredients:

For the Broth:

8 cups vegetable broth

1 large onion, peeled and halved

2 carrots, peeled and halved

2 celery stalks, halved

3 cloves garlic, smashed

1 leek, cleaned and halved

1 large potato, peeled and halved

1 turnip, peeled and halved

1 parsnip, peeled and halved

A handful of fresh parsley

2 bay leaves

Salt and pepper to taste

For the Vegan "Meatballs" (Carn d'Olla):

1 cup cooked chickpeas, mashed

1 cup cooked lentils, mashed

1/2 cup breadcrumbs

1 onion, finely chopped

2 cloves garlic, minced

1 teaspoon ground cumin

1 teaspoon smoked paprika

Salt and pepper to taste

2 tablespoons olive oil, for frying

For the Escudella:

1 cup small pasta (such as elbow or ditalini)

1 cup cooked rice

Catalan-style picada (optional, see below)

Catalan-style Picada (Optional):

A handful of almonds, toasted

A small slice of bread, toasted

2 cloves garlic

Fresh parsley, a small handful

Olive oil

Salt

Instructions:

1. Prepare the Broth:

In a large pot, combine all the broth ingredients.

Bring to a boil, then reduce the heat to low and simmer for about 1 to 1.5 hours.

Strain the broth and discard the solids, leaving a clear and flavorful broth.

2. Make the Vegan "Meatballs" (Carn d'Olla):

In a bowl, mix mashed chickpeas, lentils, breadcrumbs, chopped onion, minced garlic, cumin, smoked paprika, salt, and pepper.

Form small balls from the mixture.

Heat olive oil in a pan and fry the vegan "meatballs" until golden brown on all sides. Set aside.

3. Prepare the Catalan-style Picada (Optional):

In a food processor, combine toasted almonds, toasted bread, garlic, parsley, olive oil, and a pinch of salt.

Process until you get a coarse paste. This is the picada.

4. Assemble the Escudella i Carn d'Olla:

Bring the strained broth back to a simmer.

Cook the small pasta in the broth until al dente.

Add the cooked rice and vegan "meatballs" to the pot.

5. Serve:

Ladle the Escudella i Carn d'Olla into bowls, ensuring each serving has a mix of pasta, rice, and "meatballs."

Optionally, drizzle each serving with the Catalan-style picada for added flavor.

6. Enjoy:

Serve this comforting and hearty Vegan Escudella i Carn d'Olla with crusty bread and enjoy the warmth and flavors of Catalan cuisine.

Vegan Crema Catalana

No culinary journey through Barcelona is complete without a sweet indulgence. Enter the realm of vegan Crema Catalana, a silky dessert reminiscent of crème brûlée. Infused with citrus and cinnamon, this plant-based delight is a testament to the city's ability to reimagine classic desserts with a compassionate touch.

Ingredients:

For the Custard:

2 cups unsweetened almond milk or any plant-based milk of your choice

1/2 cup granulated sugar

Zest of 1 orange or lemon (optional)

1/2 cup cornstarch

1 teaspoon vanilla extract

A pinch of turmeric (optional, for color)

For the Caramelized Sugar Top:

1/4 cup granulated sugar

1 tablespoon water

Instructions:

1. Prepare the Custard:

In a saucepan, heat the plant-based milk over medium heat until it starts to simmer. Add the orange or lemon zest if using and stir to infuse the flavor.

In a separate bowl, whisk together sugar, cornstarch, and turmeric (if using) until well combined.

Slowly pour the sugar mixture into the simmering plant-based milk, whisking continuously to avoid lumps.

Continue whisking over medium heat until the mixture thickens and reaches a custard-like consistency. This usually takes about 5-7 minutes.

Remove the saucepan from heat and stir in the vanilla extract.

Strain the custard through a fine-mesh sieve to remove any lumps or zest.

Divide the custard among serving ramekins. Allow them to cool to room temperature before refrigerating for at least 2 hours or until fully chilled.

2. Caramelize the Sugar Top:

Once the custard has chilled, prepare the caramelized sugar topping.

In a small saucepan, combine granulated sugar and water over medium heat. Allow the sugar to dissolve without stirring.

Let the mixture simmer until it turns into a golden caramel color. Swirl the pan gently to distribute the heat evenly.

Carefully pour the caramelized sugar over the chilled custard, creating an even layer.

Allow the caramel to cool and harden, forming a crispy layer on top.

3. Serve:

Serve the Vegan Crema Catalana chilled, allowing the caramelized sugar to crack open with each spoonful.

Optionally, you can use a kitchen torch to give the sugar topping a final caramelization just before serving.

Garnish with fresh berries or mint leaves for an extra touch.

4. Enjoy:

Indulge in the creamy, caramel goodness of this Vegan Crema Catalana, a delightful and cruelty-free version of the classic Spanish dessert.

Vegan Cava Sangria

Raise a toast to Barcelona's effervescent spirit with a glass of vegan Cava Sangria. Fruits, wine, and the lively fizz of Cava create a refreshing beverage that mirrors the city's zest for life. Whether enjoyed on sun-kissed terraces or vibrant plazas, Barcelona's vegan libations capture the essence of leisure and celebration.

Ingredients:

1 bottle (750 ml) vegan Cava (Spanish sparkling wine)

1/4 cup brandy

1/4 cup orange liqueur (such as triple sec)

2 tablespoons maple syrup or agave nectar (adjust to taste)

1 orange, thinly sliced

1 lemon, thinly sliced

1 lime, thinly sliced

1 cup mixed berries (strawberries, blueberries, raspberries)

2 cups chilled sparkling water or club soda

Ice cubes

Instructions:

1. Prepare the Fruits:

Wash and slice the orange, lemon, and lime into thin rounds.

Rinse the berries and set them aside.

2. Assemble the Sangria:

In a large pitcher, combine the Cava, brandy, orange liqueur, and maple syrup or agave nectar. Stir well to combine.

Add the sliced fruits and berries to the pitcher. Mix gently to incorporate the fruits with the liquid.

Place the pitcher in the refrigerator and let the sangria chill for at least 2 hours, allowing the flavors to meld.

3. Serve:

Just before serving, add the chilled sparkling water or club soda to the sangria. Stir gently to combine.

Fill glasses with ice cubes and pour the Vegan Cava Sangria over the ice.

Garnish each glass with a few slices of fruit from the pitcher.

4. Enjoy:

Raise a glass and enjoy the effervescent and fruity goodness of Vegan Cava Sangria! It's a perfect drink for warm days, gatherings, or whenever you want to add a touch of Spanish flair to your celebrations. ¡Salud!

Culinary Fusion along the Ramblas:

Wander along the iconic La Rambla, and discover Barcelona's penchant for culinary fusion. Vegan offerings blend global influences with local ingredients, creating a tapestry of flavors that mirrors the city's cosmopolitan atmosphere. From vegan tapas to innovative plant-based dishes, the Ramblas beckon with a feast for the senses.

Ingredients:

For the Base:

2 cups cooked saffron-infused rice (prepare rice with a pinch of saffron threads)

1 cup black beans, cooked and drained

1 cup corn kernels, fresh or frozen

1 avocado, sliced

1 cup cherry tomatoes, halved

1/2 cup cucumber, diced

Fresh cilantro, chopped, for garnish

For the Spanish-Style Sofrito:

2 tablespoons olive oil

1 onion, finely chopped

2 cloves garlic, minced

1 red bell pepper, diced

1 teaspoon smoked paprika

1/2 teaspoon cumin

Salt and pepper to taste

1 cup tomato sauce

For the Tofu Chorizo:

1 block firm tofu, crumbled

1 tablespoon olive oil

1 teaspoon smoked paprika

1/2 teaspoon cumin

1/2 teaspoon chili powder

Salt and pepper to taste

For the Lime-Cilantro Dressing:

1/4 cup lime juice

2 tablespoons olive oil

1 tablespoon fresh cilantro, chopped

Salt and pepper to taste

Instructions:

1. Prepare the Spanish-Style Sofrito:

In a pan, heat olive oil over medium heat.

Add chopped onions and cook until softened.

Stir in minced garlic, diced red bell pepper, smoked paprika, cumin, salt, and pepper. Cook until the pepper is tender.

Pour in the tomato sauce and simmer for 10-15 minutes until the sofrito thickens. Set aside.

2. Make the Tofu Chorizo:

In a separate pan, heat olive oil over medium heat.

Add crumbled tofu and cook until it starts to brown.

Stir in smoked paprika, cumin, chili powder, salt, and pepper. Cook for an additional 5-7 minutes until the tofu has a chorizo-like texture.

3. Prepare the Lime-Cilantro Dressing:

Whisk together lime juice, olive oil, chopped cilantro, salt, and pepper in a small bowl.

4. Assemble the La Rambla Fusion Bowl:

In serving bowls, layer saffron-infused rice as the base.

Top with black beans, corn kernels, avocado slices, cherry tomatoes, and diced cucumber.

Spoon the Spanish-style sofrito and tofu chorizo over the rice and vegetables.

Drizzle the lime-cilantro dressing over the bowl.

Garnish with fresh cilantro.

5. Enjoy the Culinary Fusion:

Toss the La Rambla Fusion Bowl before enjoying, ensuring every bite is a delightful blend of Spanish and international flavors. This culinary fusion captures the diverse and vibrant spirit of Barcelona's famous La Rambla. ¡Buen provecho!

Conclusion:

Barcelona, with its seaside allure and artistic spirit, emerges as a haven for plant-based indulgence. In this chapter, we've navigated the city's culinary landscape, uncovering the secrets of vegan paella, reveling in the heartiness of Catalan stews, and savoring the sweetness of vegan Crema Catalana. As you savor the lingering flavors of Barcelona's plant-based delights, may this chapter be a gateway to the boundless innovation and Mediterranean charm that define this coastal jewel. ¡Buen provecho!

Seville: Traditional Flavors with a Vegan Twist

Venturing into the sun-drenched streets of Seville, where time seems to dance to the rhythm of Flamenco and the fragrance of orange blossoms fills the air, we explore a chapter dedicated to the city's timeless charm and traditional flavors. Seville, deeply rooted in Andalusian heritage, welcomes us to savor the richness of its culinary tapestry with a compassionate twist.

Vegan Salmorejo:

Our journey through Seville commences with a bowl of Vegan Salmorejo, a chilled tomato soup that embodies the essence of Andalusian summers. Bursting with the flavors of ripe tomatoes, garlic, and olive oil, this traditional dish takes on a vegan incarnation that captures the cool elegance of Seville's culinary heritage.

Ingredients:

1 kg (about 4 cups) ripe tomatoes, coarsely chopped

250g (about 2 cups) day-old bread, crust removed and torn into pieces

1 clove garlic, minced

1/4 cup extra-virgin olive oil, plus more for drizzling

2 tablespoons red wine vinegar

1 teaspoon salt, or to taste

Garnishes (optional): diced cucumber, red bell pepper, hard-boiled egg (skip for a fully vegan version)

Instructions:

1. Soak the Bread:

Place the torn bread pieces in a bowl and cover them with water. Let them soak for about 10-15 minutes.

After soaking, squeeze excess water from the bread, and set it aside.

2. Blend the Ingredients:

In a blender or food processor, combine the chopped tomatoes, soaked bread, minced garlic, olive oil, red wine vinegar, and salt.

Blend until smooth and creamy. If the soup is too thick, you can add a bit of water to reach your desired consistency.

3. Chill the Soup:

Transfer the blended mixture to a bowl or large jug.

Cover and refrigerate the soup for at least 2 hours, allowing it to chill thoroughly.

4. Serve:

Before serving, check the consistency. If it has thickened too much, you can adjust by adding a bit of water and stirring.

Serve the Vegan Salmorejo in bowls, drizzled with extra-virgin olive oil.

Optionally, garnish with diced cucumber, red bell pepper, or slices of hard-boiled egg (skip for a fully vegan version).

5. Enjoy:

Enjoy this refreshing and vegan twist on the classic Andalusian Salmorejo. It's a perfect appetizer or light meal on a hot day. Serve with crusty bread on the side for a delightful experience. ¡Buen provecho!

Espárragos de Navarra - Vegan Style

Embrace the elegance of Espárragos de Navarra, a dish that pays homage to the bounty of local asparagus. In this vegan rendition, the earthy sweetness of asparagus meets the richness of almond-based sauces, creating a symphony of flavors that reflects Seville's commitment to both tradition and innovation.

Ingredients:

1 bunch of green asparagus, trimmed

2 tablespoons olive oil

2 cloves garlic, minced

Zest of 1 lemon

Salt and pepper to taste

1 tablespoon chopped fresh parsley (for garnish)

Lemon wedges (for serving)

Instructions:

1. Prepare the Asparagus:

Trim the tough ends from the asparagus spears.

If the asparagus is thick, consider peeling the lower part for a more tender texture.

2. Blanch the Asparagus:

Bring a large pot of salted water to a boil.

Blanch the asparagus in the boiling water for 2-3 minutes, or until they are just tender but still vibrant green.

Quickly transfer the asparagus to a bowl of ice water to stop the cooking process. Once cooled, drain and pat them dry.

3. Sauté the Asparagus:

In a large skillet, heat olive oil over medium heat.

Add minced garlic and sauté for about 30 seconds, or until fragrant.

Add the blanched asparagus to the skillet.

Sauté the asparagus in the garlic-infused oil for 2-3 minutes, tossing them to coat evenly.

4. Season and Serve:

Season the asparagus with salt and pepper to taste.

Add lemon zest to the skillet and toss the asparagus to coat them in the flavors.

5. Garnish and Serve:

Transfer the sautéed asparagus to a serving plate.

Garnish with chopped fresh parsley.

Serve with lemon wedges on the side.

6. Enjoy:

Enjoy this Vegan Espárragos de Navarra as a side dish or appetizer. The simplicity of olive oil, garlic, and lemon enhances the natural flavors of the asparagus, making it a delightful and elegant dish. Serve it alongside your favorite main course for a taste of Spain. ¡Buen provecho!

Vegan Berza Gitana:

As we delve into the heartiness of Andalusian cuisine, Vegan Berza Gitana emerges as a savory revelation. This chickpea and vegetable stew, traditionally prepared with meat, transforms into a vegan masterpiece. The flavors of smoked paprika, cumin, and saffron intertwine, offering a delicious journey into the robust soul of Seville's gastronomic traditions.

Ingredients:

2 tablespoons olive oil

1 large onion, finely chopped

2 cloves garlic, minced

1 green bell pepper, diced

1 red bell pepper, diced

1 medium carrot, peeled and diced

1 medium potato, peeled and diced

1 cup green beans, chopped

1 cup diced tomatoes (fresh or canned)

1 cup chickpeas, cooked (canned or soaked and cooked)

1 cup white beans, cooked (canned or soaked and cooked)

1 teaspoon smoked paprika

1 teaspoon sweet paprika

1/2 teaspoon ground cumin

1/2 teaspoon dried oregano

1 bay leaf

Salt and pepper to taste

4 cups vegetable broth or water

1 bunch Swiss chard, kale, or collard greens, chopped

1 cup cooked rice or other grains (optional)

Lemon wedges for serving

Instructions:

1. Sauté the Vegetables:

In a large pot, heat olive oil over medium heat.

Add chopped onions and garlic, sautéing until softened.

Add diced green and red bell peppers, carrots, and potatoes. Stir well.

Cook for 5-7 minutes, allowing the vegetables to soften.

2. Add Tomatoes and Beans:

Add diced tomatoes, chickpeas, and white beans to the pot. Stir to combine.

Season with smoked paprika, sweet paprika, ground cumin, dried oregano, bay leaf, salt, and pepper. Mix well.

Pour in vegetable broth or water. Bring the mixture to a boil, then reduce the heat to low and simmer for about 20-25 minutes.

3. Incorporate Greens:

Add chopped Swiss chard, kale, or collard greens to the pot. Stir until the greens are wilted and tender.

If using, add cooked rice or other grains to the stew. Stir to combine.

4. Adjust Seasoning and Serve:

Taste the stew and adjust the seasoning if needed. Add more salt and pepper according to your preference.

Remove the bay leaf.

5. Serve:

Ladle the Vegan Berza Gitana into bowls.

Serve with lemon wedges on the side for squeezing over the stew.

6. Enjoy:

Enjoy this comforting and nourishing Vegan Berza Gitana, a delightful Spanish-inspired stew that combines the richness of vegetables and legumes. Serve it as a standalone dish or with a side of crusty bread for a complete meal. ¡Buen provecho!

Gazpacho Andaluz

No exploration of Seville's culinary landscape is complete without indulging in the refreshing elixir of Gazpacho Andaluz. This chilled soup, brimming with the brightness of tomatoes, peppers, and garlic, becomes a vibrant ode to Andalusian summers. In its vegan adaptation, Gazpacho Andaluz captivates with its simplicity and zest.

Ingredients:

6 ripe tomatoes, coarsely chopped

1 cucumber, peeled and chopped

1 green bell pepper, chopped

1 small red onion, chopped

2 cloves garlic, minced

4 cups tomato juice or vegetable broth (chilled)

1/4 cup red wine vinegar

1/4 cup extra-virgin olive oil

Salt and pepper to taste

1 teaspoon sugar (optional, to balance acidity)

Croutons, diced cucumber, and chopped fresh herbs for garnish (optional)

Instructions:

1. Prepare the Vegetables:

Coarsely chop the tomatoes, cucumber, green bell pepper, and red onion.

Mince the garlic cloves.

2. Blend the Vegetables:

In a blender or food processor, combine the chopped tomatoes, cucumber, bell pepper, red onion, and garlic.

Blend until the mixture becomes a smooth puree.

3. Season the Soup:

Add tomato juice or vegetable broth to the blender with the pureed vegetables.

Pour in red wine vinegar and extra-virgin olive oil.

Season with salt and pepper to taste. Optionally, add sugar to balance the acidity.

Blend again until all the ingredients are well combined.

4. Chill the Gazpacho:

Transfer the blended mixture to a large bowl or pitcher.

Cover and refrigerate the Gazpacho Andaluz for at least 2 hours or until well chilled.

5. Serve:

Before serving, check the seasoning and adjust if necessary.

Ladle the chilled Gazpacho into bowls.

Optionally, garnish with croutons, diced cucumber, and chopped fresh herbs.

6. Enjoy:

Enjoy the cool, refreshing flavors of Gazpacho Andaluz, a perfect soup for hot summer days. Serve it as a light appetizer or pair it with crusty bread for a delightful and nutritious meal. ¡Buen provecho!

Vegan Ajoblanco

Celebrate the cooling embrace of Vegan Ajoblanco, a traditional Andalusian almond soup. With the creaminess of almonds, the freshness of grapes, and the subtle hint of garlic, this dish exemplifies Seville's mastery in transforming simple ingredients into a symphony of flavors that transcend seasons.

Ingredients:

1 cup blanched almonds, soaked overnight

2 slices of day-old bread, crust removed

2-3 cloves garlic, peeled

1 tablespoon white wine vinegar

1/4 cup extra-virgin olive oil

2 cups cold water

Salt, to taste

Grapes or diced cucumber for garnish (optional)

Sliced almonds for garnish (optional)

Instructions:

1. Soak the Almonds:

Soak blanched almonds in water overnight or for at least 8 hours. This softens them for easier blending.

2. Prepare the Bread:

Remove the crust from the slices of day-old bread.

Tear the bread into smaller pieces.

3. Blend the Ingredients:

In a blender, combine soaked almonds, torn bread, peeled garlic cloves, white wine vinegar, and a pinch of salt.

Blend on high speed until the mixture becomes a smooth paste.

4. Add Water and Olive Oil:

With the blender running on low speed, gradually add cold water.

Continue blending and slowly drizzle in the extra-virgin olive oil.

Blend until you achieve a creamy and well-emulsified soup.

5. Adjust Seasoning:

Taste the ajoblanco and adjust the seasoning by adding more salt or vinegar if needed.

If the soup is too thick, you can add more water to reach your desired consistency.

6. Chill:

Transfer the ajoblanco to a bowl or pitcher.

Cover and refrigerate for at least 2 hours to allow the flavors to meld and the soup to chill.

7. Serve:

Before serving, stir the soup and check the consistency. If it has thickened, you can adjust with a bit of water.

Ladle the chilled ajoblanco into bowls.

Optionally, garnish with grapes or diced cucumber for a burst of freshness and sliced almonds for added texture.

8. Enjoy:

Serve this Vegan Ajoblanco as a light and cooling appetizer on warm days. Its creamy texture and subtle garlic and almond flavors make it a delightful and unique addition to your repertoire of cold soups. ¡Buen provecho!

Conclusion:

Seville, with its timeless charm and culinary authenticity, invites us to savor traditional flavors with a vegan twist. In this chapter, we've explored the cool delights of Salmorejo, the richness of Espárragos de Navarra, the heartiness of Berza Gitana, the refreshing Gazpacho Andaluz, and the creamy allure of Vegan Ajoblanco. As you turn the page, may the essence of Seville's culinary traditions linger, offering a glimpse into the city's soul and the seamless integration of vegan living into its timeless heritage. ¡Buen provecho!

Seville: Traditional Flavors with a Vegan Twist

Venturing into the sun-drenched streets of Seville, where time seems to dance to the rhythm of Flamenco and the fragrance of orange blossoms fills the air, we explore a chapter dedicated to the city's timeless charm and traditional flavors. Seville, deeply rooted in Andalusian heritage, welcomes us to savor the richness of its culinary tapestry with a compassionate twist.

Vegan Salmorejo:

Our journey through Seville commences with a bowl of Vegan Salmorejo, a chilled tomato soup that embodies the essence of Andalusian summers. Bursting with the flavors of ripe tomatoes, garlic, and olive oil, this traditional dish takes on a vegan incarnation that captures the cool elegance of Seville's culinary heritage.

Espárragos de Navarra - Vegan Style:

Embrace the elegance of Espárragos de Navarra, a dish that pays homage to the bounty of local asparagus. In this vegan rendition, the earthy sweetness of asparagus meets the richness of almond-based sauces, creating a symphony of flavors that reflects Seville's commitment to both tradition and innovation.

Vegan Berza Gitana:

As we delve into the heartiness of Andalusian cuisine, Vegan Berza Gitana emerges as a savory revelation. This chickpea and vegetable stew, traditionally prepared with meat, transforms into a vegan masterpiece. The flavors of smoked paprika, cumin, and saffron intertwine, offering a delicious journey into the robust soul of Seville's gastronomic traditions.

Gazpacho Andaluz:

No exploration of Seville's culinary landscape is complete without indulging in the refreshing elixir of Gazpacho Andaluz. This chilled soup, brimming with the brightness of tomatoes, peppers, and garlic, becomes a vibrant ode to Andalusian summers. In its vegan adaptation, Gazpacho Andaluz captivates with its simplicity and zest.

Vegan Ajoblanco:

Celebrate the cooling embrace of Vegan Ajoblanco, a traditional Andalusian almond soup. With the creaminess of almonds, the freshness of grapes, and the subtle hint of garlic, this dish exemplifies Seville's mastery in transforming simple ingredients into a symphony of flavors that transcend seasons.

Conclusion:

Seville, with its timeless charm and culinary authenticity, invites us to savor traditional flavors with a vegan twist. In this chapter, we've explored the cool delights of Salmorejo, the richness of Espárragos de Navarra, the heartiness of Berza Gitana, the refreshing Gazpacho Andaluz, and the creamy allure of Vegan Ajoblanco. As you turn the page, may the essence of Seville's culinary traditions linger, offering a glimpse into the city's soul and the seamless integration of vegan living into its timeless heritage. ¡Buen provecho!

Valencia: Culinary Adventures in Veganism

As we journey to the radiant city of Valencia, where the aroma of citrus orchards and the sounds of lively fiestas fill the air, we delve into a chapter dedicated to the culinary adventures that await in this vibrant coastal paradise. Valencia, steeped in history and famed for its gastronomic prowess, invites us to explore its plant-based delights that embody the region's zest for life.

Vegan Paella Valenciana

Our exploration begins with the crown jewel of Valencian cuisine – Vegan Paella Valenciana. Infused with the essence of saffron and the flavors of fresh vegetables, this iconic dish celebrates the region's connection to rice fields and the artistry of creating a paella that pays homage to its roots.

Ingredients:

2 cups paella rice (Bomba or Arborio)

4 cups vegetable broth

1 pinch saffron threads

1/4 cup olive oil

1 onion, finely chopped

2 bell peppers (preferably red and green), diced

2 medium tomatoes, grated

4 cloves garlic, minced

1 teaspoon smoked paprika

1 teaspoon sweet paprika

1 teaspoon ground turmeric (for color)

1 cup green beans, trimmed and cut into bite-sized pieces

1 cup artichoke hearts, quartered

1 cup chickpeas, cooked (canned or soaked and cooked)

1 lemon, cut into wedges

Salt and pepper to taste

Instructions:

1. Infuse Saffron:

In a small bowl, combine saffron threads with a couple of tablespoons of warm water. Let it infuse for about 15-20 minutes.

2. Prepare Vegetable Broth:

Heat the vegetable broth in a saucepan. Once warm, add the infused saffron and let it steep.

3. Sauté Vegetables:

In a large paella pan or a wide, shallow skillet, heat olive oil over medium heat.

Add chopped onions and bell peppers. Sauté until softened.

Add minced garlic and cook for another minute until fragrant.

4. Add Tomatoes and Spices:

Grate the tomatoes directly into the pan, discarding the skins. Stir well.

Add smoked paprika, sweet paprika, ground turmeric, salt, and pepper. Mix to combine.

5. Incorporate Rice:

Add paella rice to the pan, stirring to coat it with the vegetable mixture.

Let the rice toast for a couple of minutes, ensuring it's well coated with the flavors.

6. Pour in Broth:

Strain the saffron-infused vegetable broth into the pan. Discard the saffron threads.

Stir well to distribute the ingredients evenly.

7. Add Vegetables and Chickpeas:

Arrange green beans, artichoke hearts, and chickpeas evenly across the pan.

8. Cook:

Reduce the heat to low and let the paella simmer gently. Avoid stirring too much; paella forms a delicious crust, called "socarrat," at the bottom.

Cook for about 20-25 minutes or until the rice is tender and has absorbed the liquid. Add more broth if needed.

9. Finish and Serve:

Once the rice is cooked, remove the paella from heat and let it rest for a few minutes.

Squeeze lemon wedges over the paella and serve directly from the pan.

10. Enjoy:

Serve this Vegan Paella Valenciana as a flavorful and satisfying one-pan dish. The combination of saffron, vegetables, and chickpeas captures the essence of traditional paella in a vegan-friendly way. ¡Buen provecho!

Vegan All i Pebre

Embark on a journey into the heartiness of Valencian stews with Vegan All i Pebre. Traditionally a fisherman's dish, this plant-based adaptation captures the robust flavors of garlic, paprika, and potatoes, creating a culinary adventure that mirrors the region's historical ties to the sea.

Ingredients:

2 cups mushrooms (such as oyster or king trumpet), sliced

1 cup potatoes, peeled and cut into chunks

1 head of garlic, cloves peeled and minced

1 onion, finely chopped

2 tablespoons olive oil

1 tablespoon sweet paprika

1 teaspoon smoked paprika

1 bay leaf

A pinch of saffron threads

Salt and pepper to taste

1.5 liters vegetable broth

Fresh parsley, chopped (for garnish)

1 slice of rustic bread per serving (optional)

Instructions:

1. Sauté Mushrooms:

In a large pot or paella pan, heat olive oil over medium heat.

Add sliced mushrooms and sauté until they start to brown.

2. Add Onion and Garlic:

Add finely chopped onion and minced garlic to the pot. Sauté until the onion is translucent.

3. Add Paprika and Saffron:

Stir in sweet paprika and smoked paprika, coating the mushrooms, onion, and garlic.

Add a pinch of saffron threads and the bay leaf. Mix well.

4. Add Potatoes and Broth:

Add the potato chunks to the pot and stir to combine.

Pour in vegetable broth, ensuring that the potatoes are mostly submerged.

5. Simmer:

Bring the mixture to a boil, then reduce the heat to low.

Let it simmer gently until the potatoes are tender and the flavors meld, typically around 25-30 minutes.

6. Adjust Seasoning:

Season with salt and pepper to taste. Adjust the paprika or other seasonings if needed.

7. Serve:

Ladle the Vegan All i Pebre into bowls.

Garnish with chopped fresh parsley.

8. Optional Bread:

For a traditional touch, you can serve each bowl with a slice of rustic bread to soak up the delicious broth.

9. Enjoy:

Savor the rich flavors of this Vegan All i Pebre, a comforting and hearty dish with a plant-based twist. The combination of mushrooms, potatoes, and aromatic spices makes for a satisfying and flavorful meal. ¡Buen provecho!

Vegan Fideuà Marinera

Celebrate the ocean's bounty with Vegan Fideuà Marinera, a dish that mirrors the flavors of paella but with a delectable twist. In this plant-based rendition, pasta replaces rice, creating a delightful fusion of textures and tastes that exemplify Valencia's innovative approach to culinary exploration.

Ingredients:

200g (about 2 cups) fideuà noodles (short, thin noodles)

2 tablespoons olive oil

1 onion, finely chopped

2 cloves garlic, minced

1 red bell pepper, diced

1 green bell pepper, diced

1 medium tomato, grated

1 teaspoon smoked paprika

1/2 teaspoon saffron threads

1 bay leaf

1 cup mixed plant-based seafood alternatives (such as vegan shrimp, calamari, or scallops)

4 cups vegetable broth

Salt and pepper to taste

Fresh parsley, chopped (for garnish)

Lemon wedges (for serving)

Instructions:

1. Prepare the Vegetable Broth:

In a saucepan, heat the vegetable broth over medium heat. Add saffron threads and a bay leaf, allowing them to infuse into the broth.

2. Sauté Vegetables:

In a large paella pan or wide skillet, heat olive oil over medium heat.

Add chopped onion and minced garlic. Sauté until softened.

Add diced red and green bell peppers. Cook until the peppers are tender.

3. Add Grated Tomato and Paprika:

Grate the tomato directly into the pan, discarding the skins.

Stir in smoked paprika, mixing well to combine.

4. Incorporate Plant-Based Seafood Alternatives:

Add the plant-based seafood alternatives to the pan. Stir and let them cook for a few minutes to absorb the flavors.

5. Add Fideuà Noodles:

Add the fideuà noodles to the pan, stirring to coat them in the vegetable mixture.

Toast the noodles for a couple of minutes until they become golden brown.

6. Pour in Vegetable Broth:

Strain the infused vegetable broth into the pan, discarding the saffron threads and bay leaf.

Season with salt and pepper to taste. Be mindful of the saltiness of the plant-based seafood alternatives.

7. Simmer:

Reduce the heat to low and let the fideuà simmer gently. Avoid stirring too much to allow a crust, called "socarrat," to form at the bottom.

Cook for about 10-15 minutes or until the noodles are cooked and have absorbed the liquid.

8. Finish and Serve:

Once the fideuà is cooked, remove it from heat and let it rest for a few minutes.

Garnish with chopped fresh parsley.

9. Serve with Lemon Wedges:

Serve the Vegan Fideuà Marinera with lemon wedges on the side for squeezing over the dish.

10. Enjoy:

Indulge in the delightful flavors of this Vegan Fideuà Marinera, a plant-based twist on a classic Spanish dish. The combination of savory noodles, vegetables, and plant-based seafood creates a satisfying and flavorful meal. ¡Buen provecho!

Agua de Valencia

Raise a glass to the spirit of festivity with a sip of Agua de Valencia, a cocktail that encapsulates the vivacious atmosphere of Valencia. Bursting with the effervescence of Cava, orange juice, vodka, and gin, this vegan libation is a toast to the city's love for celebration and the joyous moments that define Valencian life.

Ingredients:

2 cups freshly squeezed orange juice

1 cup vegan sparkling wine or cava

1/4 cup vodka

1/4 cup gin

2 tablespoons agave syrup or simple syrup (adjust to taste)

Ice cubes

Orange slices or twists for garnish

Instructions:

1. Squeeze Orange Juice:

Freshly squeeze oranges to obtain 2 cups of orange juice. Ensure it's strained to remove any pulp or seeds.

2. Mix the Cocktail:

In a large pitcher, combine the freshly squeezed orange juice, vegan sparkling wine or cava, vodka, and gin.

Add agave syrup or simple syrup to sweeten the cocktail. Adjust the sweetness according to your preference.

Stir the mixture well to ensure the ingredients are fully combined.

3. Chill:

Refrigerate the mixture for at least 1-2 hours to allow the flavors to meld and the cocktail to chill.

4. Serve:

Fill glasses with ice cubes.

Pour the chilled Agua de Valencia into the glasses.

5. Garnish:

Garnish each glass with a slice or twist of orange for a decorative touch.

6. Enjoy:

Sip and enjoy the lively and citrusy flavors of this Vegan Agua de Valencia. It's a perfect cocktail for festive occasions or simply to cool down on a warm day. ¡Salud!

Culinary Abundance in Mercado Central

Wander through the bustling aisles of Mercado Central, Valencia's historic market, and discover a treasure trove of plant-based ingredients. From fresh produce to local delicacies, this chapter unveils the culinary abundance that awaits in the heart of the city, where veganism seamlessly integrates into the vibrant tapestry of Valencian life.

Mercado Central Bounty Bowl:

Ingredients:

For the Base:

2 cups quinoa, cooked

1 can (15 oz) black beans, drained and rinsed

1 cup cherry tomatoes, halved

1 cucumber, diced

1 avocado, sliced

1 cup corn kernels, fresh or frozen (cooked if using frozen)

1 cup shredded purple cabbage

Fresh cilantro, chopped (for garnish)

For the Dressing:

3 tablespoons olive oil

Juice of 1 lime

1 tablespoon balsamic vinegar

1 teaspoon Dijon mustard

Salt and pepper to taste

Instructions:

1. Assemble the Base:

In a large bowl, combine cooked quinoa, black beans, cherry tomatoes, diced cucumber, avocado slices, corn kernels, and shredded purple cabbage.

2. Prepare the Dressing:

In a small bowl, whisk together olive oil, lime juice, balsamic vinegar, Dijon mustard, salt, and pepper.

Pour the dressing over the ingredients in the large bowl.

3. Toss and Garnish:

Gently toss the ingredients to coat them evenly with the dressing.

Garnish the bowl with fresh cilantro.

4. Serve:

Divide the Mercado Central Bounty Bowl into individual servings.

Optionally, you can add a protein of your choice, such as grilled tofu, tempeh, or plant-based meat alternatives.

5. Enjoy:

Savor the abundance of flavors and textures in this Mercado Central-inspired bowl. The combination of fresh vegetables, quinoa, and a zesty dressing creates a colorful and nutritious dish that celebrates the variety found in a bustling market. ¡Buen provecho!

Conclusion:

Valencia, with its culinary adventures and zestful spirit, emerges as a haven for plant-based exploration. In this chapter, we've savored the iconic Vegan Paella Valenciana, delved into the heartiness of Vegan All i Pebre and Fideuà Marinera, raised a glass of Agua de Valencia, and explored the culinary abundance of Mercado Central. As you immerse yourself in the flavors of Valencia, may this chapter be a celebration of the city's vibrant gastronomic landscape and its seamless embrace of plant-based living. ¡Buen provecho!

Granada: Exploring Vegan Tapas

Our culinary journey now leads us to the enchanting city of Granada, where the echoes of Moorish history linger in the Alhambra's walls, and the charm of cobblestone streets beckons us to discover the art of tapas. In this chapter, we explore Granada's vibrant tapas culture and the innovative plant-based creations that elevate the city's culinary scene.

Vegan Papas a lo Pobre

Begin your tapas adventure in Granada with the savory delight of Vegan Papas a lo Pobre. Traditionally made with potatoes, green peppers, and onions, this vegan rendition captures the essence of Andalusian comfort food. Served hot and drizzled with olive oil, it's a flavorful introduction to Granada's tapas tradition.

Ingredients:

4 large potatoes, peeled and sliced into thin rounds

1 large onion, thinly sliced

1 green bell pepper, thinly sliced

1 red bell pepper, thinly sliced

3 cloves garlic, minced

1/4 cup olive oil

1 teaspoon sweet paprika

Salt and pepper to taste

Chopped fresh parsley for garnish

Instructions:

1. Prepare the Potatoes:

Peel the potatoes and slice them into thin rounds.

2. Sauté the Vegetables:

In a large skillet or pan, heat olive oil over medium heat.

Add the sliced potatoes, onions, and peppers to the pan.

Sauté the vegetables until the potatoes are golden brown and cooked through, and the onions and peppers are soft.

3. Add Garlic and Seasonings:

Add minced garlic to the pan and sauté for an additional 1-2 minutes until fragrant.

Sprinkle sweet paprika over the potatoes and vegetables. Season with salt and pepper to taste.

4. Cook until Tender:

Continue to cook, stirring occasionally, until the potatoes are fully tender and have absorbed the flavors of the onions, peppers, and garlic.

5. Garnish and Serve:

Once the potatoes are cooked, transfer them to a serving dish.

Garnish with chopped fresh parsley for a burst of color and added freshness.

6. Enjoy:

Serve these Vegan Papas a lo Pobre as a delightful side dish or a simple and satisfying main course. The combination of tender potatoes, sweet onions, and colorful peppers creates a dish that is both comforting and flavorful. ¡Buen provecho!

Vegan Almond Soup

Indulge in the velvety texture of Vegan Almond Soup, a dish that embodies the richness of Moorish influences in Granada's gastronomy. Infused with the nutty flavors of almonds, garlic, and olive oil, this cold soup is a testament to the city's ability to transform simple ingredients into a culinary masterpiece.

Ingredients:

1 cup blanched almonds, soaked overnight

2 slices of day-old bread, crust removed

2 cloves garlic, minced

2 tablespoons white wine vinegar

1/4 cup extra-virgin olive oil

2 cups cold water

Salt, to taste

Grapes or diced cucumber for garnish (optional)

Sliced almonds for garnish (optional)

Instructions:

1. Soak the Almonds:

Soak blanched almonds in water overnight or for at least 8 hours. This helps soften them for blending.

2. Prepare the Bread:

Remove the crust from the slices of day-old bread.

Tear the bread into smaller pieces.

3. Blend the Ingredients:

In a blender, combine soaked almonds, torn bread, minced garlic, white wine vinegar, and a pinch of salt.

Blend on high speed until the mixture becomes a smooth paste.

4. Add Water and Olive Oil:

With the blender running on low speed, gradually add cold water.

Continue blending and slowly drizzle in the extra-virgin olive oil.

Blend until you achieve a creamy and well-emulsified soup.

5. Adjust Seasoning:

Taste the soup and add more salt if needed. You can also adjust the consistency by adding more water if it's too thick.

6. Chill:

Transfer the soup to a bowl or pitcher.

Cover and refrigerate for at least 2 hours or until well chilled.

7. Serve:

Before serving, stir the soup and check the consistency. Adjust with a bit of water if necessary.

Ladle the chilled Vegan Almond Soup into bowls.

8. Garnish:

Garnish with grapes or diced cucumber for a burst of freshness and sliced almonds for added texture.

9. Enjoy:

Savor the unique and delightful flavors of this Vegan Almond Soup. It's a perfect cold soup for warmer days, and the combination of almonds, garlic, and olive oil creates a rich and satisfying experience. ¡Buen provecho!

Vegan Zanahorias Aliñadas

Savor the sweetness of carrots in Vegan Zanahorias Aliñadas, a tapa that celebrates the bounty of fresh produce. Marinated in a delightful blend of olive oil, garlic, and vinegar, this vegan tapa showcases Granada's commitment to highlighting the natural flavors of vegetables.

Ingredients:

4 large carrots, peeled and sliced into thin rounds

2 cloves garlic, minced

2 tablespoons fresh parsley, chopped

2 tablespoons red wine vinegar

4 tablespoons extra-virgin olive oil

1 teaspoon ground cumin

1 teaspoon sweet paprika

Salt and pepper to taste

Instructions:

1. Prepare the Carrots:

Peel the carrots and slice them into thin rounds.

2. Steam the Carrots:

Steam the carrot rounds until they are just tender. This should take about 5-7 minutes. You want them to be cooked but still have a bit of crunch.

3. Prepare the Marinade:

In a bowl, combine minced garlic, chopped parsley, red wine vinegar, extra-virgin olive oil, ground cumin, sweet paprika, salt, and pepper. Mix well.

4. Marinate the Carrots:

Place the steamed carrot rounds in a shallow dish.

Pour the marinade over the carrots, ensuring they are well coated.

Gently toss the carrots to distribute the marinade evenly.

Allow the carrots to marinate for at least 30 minutes, or refrigerate for a couple of hours to let the flavors meld.

5. Serve:

Once marinated, transfer the Vegan Zanahorias Aliñadas to a serving dish.

Garnish with additional parsley if desired.

6. Enjoy:

Serve this flavorful and colorful dish as a side or tapa. The combination of the marinated carrots with garlic, cumin, and paprika creates a vibrant and tasty experience. ¡Buen provecho!

The Charm of Vegan Tapas Bars:

Granada's vibrant tapas bars, nestled in the labyrinthine streets of the Albaicín and Realejo districts, become the stage for culinary exploration. This chapter unveils the charm of these establishments, where vegan options seamlessly integrate into the tapestry of traditional offerings, creating a diverse and inclusive tapas experience.

Vegan Tapas Culture:

Delve into the heart of Granada's tapas culture, where the act of sharing small plates becomes a social ritual. From olives to marinated vegetables, the vegan offerings are a celebration of the city's commitment to inclusivity and the belief that everyone should savor the pleasures of tapas, regardless of dietary choices.

Conclusion:

Granada, with its historic charm and culinary allure, emerges as a haven for exploring vegan tapas. In this chapter, we've relished the delights of Vegan Papas a lo Pobre, immersed ourselves in the richness of Vegan Almond Soup, and celebrated the freshness of Vegan Zanahorias Aliñadas. As you navigate Granada's tapas bars and embrace the social art of sharing plates, may this chapter be a joyful exploration of the city's vibrant vegan tapas culture. ¡Buen provecho!

Chapter 4: Vegan-Friendly Accommodations: A Haven for Plant-Based Travelers

In the ever-evolving landscape of travel, finding accommodations that align with a plant-based lifestyle has become a pivotal aspect of the modern journey. This chapter unfolds as a comprehensive guide, navigating the realms of vegan-friendly lodgings, from eco-conscious boutique hotels to sustainable resorts that not only cater to the needs of plant-based travelers but actively embrace the ethos of cruelty-free living.

The Rise of Vegan-Friendly Lodgings:

As the demand for vegan-friendly options continues to surge, accommodations worldwide are adapting to this transformative shift in travel preferences. Explore the roots of this movement, understanding how the rise of veganism has catalyzed a new era of hospitality, one that prioritizes ethical considerations, sustainability, and the well-being of both guests and the planet.

Criteria for Vegan-Friendly Accommodations:

Embark on a journey through the criteria that define vegan-friendly accommodations. From cruelty-free toiletries and plant-based dining options to eco-conscious practices, this section equips travelers with the knowledge to discern lodgings that align with their values. Delve into the nuances of what makes an accommodation truly vegan-friendly and discover how these considerations extend beyond the plate.

Eco-Conscious Boutique Hotels:

Enter the realm of eco-conscious boutique hotels, where sustainability and luxury coalesce to offer a distinctive lodging experience. From minimalist design to locally sourced amenities, explore how these accommodations prioritize environmental responsibility without compromising on style and comfort. Uncover the nuances of eco-friendly practices that make these boutique hotels a haven for conscious travelers.

Sustainable Resorts with a Vegan Touch:

Journey to sustainable resorts that go beyond environmental stewardship to actively embrace plant-based living. Delve into the culinary offerings, wellness programs, and eco-initiatives that make these resorts a sanctuary for vegan travelers. Whether nestled in tropical landscapes or perched on mountain vistas, these sustainable havens redefine luxury with a compassionate touch.

Cruelty-Free Accommodations in Urban Landscapes:

Navigate the bustling urban landscapes, discovering cruelty-free accommodations in the heart of cities. From vegan room service to ethical design principles, these lodgings seamlessly integrate plant-based considerations into the urban traveler's experience. Learn how vegan-friendly options in urban settings cater to the needs of those seeking conscious and compassionate stays.

Vegan Retreats and Wellness Centers:

Immerse yourself in the serenity of vegan retreats and wellness centers that prioritize holistic well-being. From yoga retreats with plant-based menus to wellness centers promoting cruelty-free beauty treatments, this section unravels the diverse offerings that make these havens a respite for travelers seeking rejuvenation, mindfulness, and a compassionate escape.

Case Studies: Exemplars of Vegan-Friendly Accommodations:

Embark on a virtual tour through case studies that spotlight exemplars of vegan-friendly accommodations. From innovative initiatives to success stories, these real-world examples showcase how lodgings are adapting to the growing demand for plant-based options, enriching the traveler's experience and fostering a more sustainable and compassionate approach to hospitality.

Conclusion: A Future of Vegan-Friendly Hospitality:

As we conclude this exploration into vegan-friendly accommodations, envision the future of hospitality that awaits. From boutique hotels to sustainable resorts, the trajectory is clear – a future where plant-based travelers can seamlessly integrate their lifestyle choices into every aspect of their journeys. Celebrate the evolution of travel and hospitality, where vegan-friendly accommodations not only meet expectations but exceed them, promising a stay that aligns with values and contributes to a more compassionate and sustainable world.

Chapter 5: Farmers' Markets and Local Produce

Embark on a sensory journey through the vibrant tapestry of local flavors and culinary traditions as we explore the bountiful world of farmers' markets and local produce. This chapter is a celebration of the intersection between plant-based living and the agricultural landscapes of travel destinations, where the richness of local ingredients becomes a palette for culinary exploration.

Step into the heart of bustling farmers' markets, where the air is infused with the aroma of fresh produce, artisanal crafts, and the lively chatter of local vendors. Explore the essence of these markets as communal hubs, not only for sourcing ingredients but for immersing in the cultural fabric of a destination. Uncover the unique character each market contributes to the culinary landscape.

Navigate the labyrinthine stalls and vibrant displays as a vegan traveler, discovering the treasures that farmers' markets hold for plant-based diets. From seasonal fruits and vegetables to locally sourced pantry staples, this section provides insights into making the most of your market experience. Learn to decode labels, interact with vendors, and uncover hidden gems that align with your plant-based preferences.

Exploring Fresh and Local Ingredients: A Culinary Odyssey

Embark on a culinary odyssey as we delve into the heart of exploring fresh and local ingredients. This chapter is a sensory exploration, guiding the vegan traveler through markets, farms, and local purveyors, unveiling the essence of regional flavors and the artistry of plant-based cuisine inspired by the bounties of each destination.

The Culinary Palette of Freshness:

Discover the transformative power of freshness as the culinary palette unfolds before you. From vibrant fruits to crisp vegetables, the journey into exploring fresh and local ingredients is a celebration of nature's abundance. Uncover the nuances of seasonality, understanding how each region paints its culinary canvas with a kaleidoscope of flavors throughout the year.

Market Wanderlust:

Stroll through bustling markets where the air is alive with the aromas of herbs, spices, and the vibrant hues of fresh produce. This section is a guide to cultivating market wanderlust, where each stall tells a story of local agriculture, culinary traditions, and the tapestry of flavors waiting to be woven into your plant-based creations.

Farm-to-Table Adventures:

Embark on farm-to-table adventures that transcend the restaurant experience. Dive into the heart of local farms, orchards, and sustainable agricultural practices. Learn the art of ethical sourcing, meeting farmers, and understanding the journey of ingredients from the field to your plate. This section is an invitation to savor the authenticity and traceability that comes with every farm-to-table encounter.

Local Artisans and Producers:

Meet the artisans and producers who infuse passion into their craft. From small-batch producers of olive oil to masterful bakers creating plant-based delights, this exploration is a tribute to the skilled hands behind the local ingredients that elevate your culinary experiences. Understand the stories behind the products and the dedication to quality that defines these local treasures.

Culinary Workshops and Cooking Classes:

Immerse yourself in the art of plant-based cooking through culinary workshops and cooking classes. Join local chefs in hands-on experiences that showcase the brilliance of fresh and local ingredients. Learn the techniques, flavor combinations, and cultural influences that transform a handful of local produce into a symphony of tastes on your plate.

Seasonal Inspirations:

Explore the beauty of cooking with the seasons, discovering how regional climates shape the culinary calendar. From the earthy warmth of autumn to the vibrant freshness of spring, this section is an ode to seasonal inspirations that guide your culinary creativity. Learn to adapt your plant-based recipes to the ever-changing bounty of local harvests.

Case Studies: Culinary Excellence with Local Ingredients:

Delve into case studies that spotlight culinary excellence with local ingredients. Explore examples where chefs, home cooks, and culinary influencers showcase the versatility of fresh, regional produce in creating remarkable plant-based dishes. These case studies offer insights into how local ingredients can be the stars of extraordinary culinary creations.

Conclusion: Crafting Culinary Memories with Local Bounty:

As you conclude this culinary odyssey, savor the memories crafted with each bite of fresh and local ingredients. This chapter is a testament to the richness that unfolds when you embrace the local bounty, allowing regional flavors to shape your plant-based journey. Celebrate the artistry of plant-based cuisine inspired by the landscapes, cultures, and communities that generously share their freshness with every plate.

Chapter 6: Vegan-Friendly Festivals and Events: Celebrating Compassion and Culture

Embark on a journey through the kaleidoscope of vegan-friendly festivals and events, where compassion converges with culture, and plant-based living takes center stage. This chapter is a celebration of the diverse gatherings around the world that unite communities, showcase culinary artistry, and embody the spirit of conscious living.

The Global Tapestry of Vegan Festivals:

Unravel the global tapestry of vegan festivals, from the pulsating energy of street fairs to the sophistication of culinary showcases. This section introduces you to the vibrant array of events that span continents, each with its unique blend of flavors, traditions, and a shared commitment to the ethical and sustainable lifestyle.

Culinary Extravaganzas:

Dive into culinary extravaganzas where the world of plant-based cuisine unfolds in all its glory. Explore how vegan festivals and events serve as platforms for chefs, food entrepreneurs, and culinary enthusiasts to showcase their talents. From artisanal vegan cheeses to innovative plant-based desserts, these gatherings redefine the boundaries of vegan gastronomy.

Ethical Fashion and Lifestyle Expos:

Celebrate the intersection of compassion and style in vegan-friendly festivals that spotlight ethical fashion and lifestyle. From cruelty-free fashion shows to sustainable living expos, these events showcase a holistic approach to conscious living, proving that compassion extends beyond the plate to every facet of our daily lives.

Animal Rights Activism and Awareness:

Immerse yourself in the activism and awareness campaigns that take center stage in vegan festivals. Learn how these events become platforms for raising awareness about animal rights, fostering compassion, and inspiring change. From engaging talks to interactive exhibits, discover the myriad ways in which these festivals contribute to a more compassionate world.

Yoga and Wellness Retreats:

Embark on vegan-friendly festivals that transcend gastronomy, delving into the realms of wellness and mindfulness. Explore how yoga and wellness retreats, often aligned with vegan principles, provide spaces for rejuvenation, self-discovery, and a deeper connection to a compassionate lifestyle.

Live Performances and Cultural Celebrations:

Witness the fusion of veganism with art, music, and cultural celebrations. From live performances by vegan musicians to cultural festivals that celebrate plant-based living, this section explores how creativity and culture become powerful tools in spreading the message of compassion and ethical living.

DIY and Sustainable Living Workshops:

Participate in DIY and sustainable living workshops that empower attendees to adopt a more eco-friendly and ethical lifestyle. From crafting cruelty-free beauty products to learning about zero-waste practices, these festivals provide practical insights and skills for incorporating sustainability into daily life.

Case Studies: Pinnacles of Vegan Festival Excellence:

Delve into case studies that showcase the pinnacles of vegan festival excellence. Explore examples where festivals have become transformative forces in promoting plant-based living, building communities, and leaving a lasting impact on individuals and societies.

Conclusion: A Tapestry Woven in Compassion and Celebration:

As you conclude this exploration of vegan-friendly festivals and events, celebrate the tapestry woven in compassion and celebration. Whether you're a seasoned festival-goer or a newcomer to the vibrant world of vegan gatherings, may this chapter inspire you to partake in the global movement towards a more compassionate and sustainable future.

Celebrating Veganism Across Spain: A Culinary Voyage

Embark on a culinary voyage through the diverse landscapes of Spain, where the essence of veganism is celebrated with every bite. This chapter is a tribute to the flourishing vegan movement across the country, from the heart of Madrid to the coastal delights of Barcelona, the cultural haven of Seville, the vibrant streets of Valencia, and the enchanting alleys of Granada.

Madrid: A Vegan Gastronomic Haven:

Discover Madrid as a vegan gastronomic haven, where the historic plazas and modern districts alike embrace plant-based dining. From traditional tapas bars offering vegan twists to avant-garde restaurants redefining culinary boundaries, this section is a culinary journey through the Spanish capital, celebrating the diversity and innovation of Madrid's vegan scene.

Barcelona: Plant-Based Delights by the Sea:

Navigate the coastal city of Barcelona, where plant-based delights harmonize with the sea breeze. Explore the beachside promenades adorned with vegan eateries, from classic paella with a plant-based twist to avant-garde creations that mirror the artistic spirit of the city. This section is an ode to Barcelona's fusion of culinary traditions and modern innovation.

Seville: Traditional Flavors with a Vegan Twist:

Immerse yourself in the traditional flavors of Seville, where the legacy of Andalusian cuisine meets the evolving landscape of plant-based living. From Vegan Salmorejo to Espárragos de Navarra, this chapter celebrates Seville's ability to infuse vegan twists into timeless classics, creating a culinary tapestry that reflects the city's cultural richness.

Valencia: Culinary Adventures in Veganism:

Explore the culinary adventures that unfold in Valencia, a city that embraces plant-based living with a zestful spirit. From the iconic Vegan Paella Valenciana to refreshing Agua de Valencia, Valencia's vegan offerings mirror the vibrancy of its festivals and the abundant harvests of its fertile landscapes.

Granada: Exploring Vegan Tapas:

Stroll through the enchanting streets of Granada, where the tradition of tapas meets the innovation of vegan cuisine. From Vegan Papas a lo Pobre to Vegan Almond Soup, this section captures the essence of Granada's vegan tapas culture, inviting you to savor the flavors that emanate from the historic Albaicín and Realejo districts.

Case Studies: Vegan Success Stories in Spanish Cities:

Delve into case studies that spotlight vegan success stories in Spanish cities. Explore how individuals, restaurants, and communities have championed the cause of plant-based living, creating a more inclusive and diverse culinary landscape. These case studies showcase the transformative power of veganism in shaping the gastronomic narratives of Spain.

Conclusion: A Tapestry of Vegan Delights Across Spain:

As you conclude this culinary voyage through Spain, savor the tapestry of vegan delights woven across its cities. Whether you're indulging in Madrid's gastronomic innovations, relishing Barcelona's seaside offerings, embracing Seville's traditional twists, embarking on culinary adventures in Valencia, or exploring the tapas culture of Granada, may this chapter be an invitation to celebrate the diverse and vibrant vegan movement thriving across Spain. ¡Buen provecho!

Chapter 7: Cooking Classes and Culinary Tours

Immerse yourself in the art of culinary exploration, where cooking classes and culinary tours become portals to the soul of a destination. From bustling markets to intimate kitchens, this section unveils the transformative power of hands-on experiences, inviting you to not just taste, but actively participate in the creation of regional delicacies.

Experience the joy of hands-on learning as you chop, sauté, and simmer your way through cooking classes that cater to plant-based diets. This section provides insights into how these classes go beyond recipes, fostering a deeper understanding of techniques, flavor profiles, and the cultural significance of each dish.

Embark on culinary tours that offer a feast for the senses. From guided market excursions to visits to local farms, these tours immerse you in the terroir of a region, allowing you to witness the journey of ingredients from field to plate. Explore how culinary tours become sensory experiences that go beyond taste, incorporating sight, smell, and touch.

Embark on a culinary masterclass as we delve
into the art of vegan Spanish cooking. This
chapter is an immersive journey into the heart
of Spain's gastronomic traditions, where plant-
based ingredients take center stage, creating a
tapestry of flavors that pays homage to the rich
culinary heritage of the Iberian Peninsula.

The Essence of Spanish Culinary Heritage:

Immerse yourself in the essence of Spanish
culinary heritage, where centuries-old traditions
meet the innovation of plant-based living. This
section introduces you to the key elements that
define the art of vegan Spanish cooking, from
the use of olive oil and aromatic spices to the
celebration of fresh, seasonal produce.

Mastering Vegan Tapas:

Delve into the intricate art of crafting vegan tapas, where small plates become a canvas for culinary creativity. From traditional favorites with a plant-based twist to innovative creations inspired by Spain's diverse regions, learn the techniques and flavor combinations that elevate vegan tapas to an art form.

Iconic Spanish Dishes Reinvented:

Explore iconic Spanish dishes reinvented for the plant-based palate. Whether it's a vegan interpretation of Paella Valenciana or a cruelty-free take on Patatas Bravas, this section guides you through the process of preserving the essence of traditional Spanish dishes while embracing the principles of plant-based cooking.

Savoring Seasonal Delights:

Celebrate the beauty of seasonal ingredients in vegan Spanish cuisine. From the bounty of summer tomatoes in Gazpacho to the hearty winter stews, this chapter explores how the culinary calendar shapes the flavors of Spanish dishes. Learn to adapt recipes to the seasons, creating dishes that mirror the vibrancy of Spain's diverse landscapes.

Infusing Spanish Flavors into Global Cuisine:

Expand your culinary repertoire by infusing Spanish flavors into global plant-based dishes. This section explores how the bold tastes of Spain can enhance a variety of cuisines, from Mediterranean-inspired salads to fusion creations that seamlessly blend the diverse influences of Spanish gastronomy.

Wine and Dining: Perfect Pairings for Vegan Delights:

Delight in the art of pairing vegan Spanish dishes with the perfect wines. From robust reds that complement rich stews to crisp whites that enhance the freshness of salads, this chapter explores the nuanced world of vegan wine and dining, elevating your culinary experiences to a symphony of tastes.

Cooking Tips and Techniques: Secrets from Spanish Kitchens:

Navigate the secrets from Spanish kitchens with practical cooking tips and techniques. Learn how to achieve the perfect sauté, the art of seasoning with Spanish spices, and the secrets to creating the ideal texture in plant-based dishes. This section equips you with the skills to recreate the authenticity of Spanish flavors in your home kitchen.

Case Studies: Culinary Mastery in Vegan Spanish Cooking:

Delve into case studies that showcase culinary mastery in vegan Spanish cooking. Explore examples where chefs, cooking schools, and culinary influencers demonstrate innovative approaches, successful adaptations, and a commitment to preserving the essence of Spanish culinary traditions in plant-based dishes.

Conclusion: A Culinary Masterclass to Remember:

As you conclude this culinary masterclass in vegan Spanish cooking, savor the flavors that have graced your kitchen. May this chapter be an inspiration to continue honing your skills, exploring the depths of plant-based Spanish cuisine, and creating memorable dishes that pay homage to the rich culinary tapestry of Spain. ¡Buen provecho!

Chapter 8: Vegan Spain Beyond the Plate

Embark on a multifaceted exploration as we venture beyond the plate into the realms of culture, lifestyle, and activism in vegan Spain. This chapter is a testament to the vibrant tapestry woven by the vegan movement, influencing not only what we eat but also how we live, celebrate, and advocate for a more compassionate world.

Vegan Fashion and Beauty:

Discover the intersection of veganism with fashion and beauty, where cruelty-free practices and ethical choices redefine personal style. From sustainable fashion brands to vegan beauty products, this section explores how Spain's growing vegan movement extends beyond the kitchen, shaping the choices we make in what we wear and how we care for ourselves.

Vegan Festivals and Events: Beyond Culinary Celebrations:

Dive into the rich tapestry of vegan festivals and events that extend beyond culinary celebrations. From eco-conscious fashion shows to wellness expos promoting plant-based living, this chapter showcases how the vegan ethos permeates diverse aspects of life, fostering a holistic approach to conscious living.

Eco-Friendly Practices: Nurturing a Sustainable Tomorrow

Embark on a journey into the realm of eco-friendly practices in Spain, where sustainability becomes a guiding principle for individuals, businesses, and communities. This chapter is a celebration of mindful living, offering insights into how eco-friendly practices contribute to the preservation of the environment and the well-being of our planet.

Green Initiatives in Urban Spaces:

Explore the green initiatives transforming urban spaces across Spain. From rooftop gardens in Madrid to community parks in Barcelona, this section unveils how cities are embracing eco-friendly practices to create more sustainable and livable environments. Discover how green spaces contribute to biodiversity, air quality, and the overall well-being of urban dwellers.

Sustainable Agriculture and Farming:

Delve into the world of sustainable agriculture and farming practices that shape Spain's food landscape. From organic vineyards in La Rioja to regenerative farming in Andalusia, this chapter explores how farmers are adopting eco-friendly methods that prioritize soil health, biodiversity, and ethical treatment of animals.

Zero-Waste Living:

Embark on a journey into zero-waste living, where individuals and businesses in Spain are minimizing their environmental footprint. From bulk stores in Valencia to community-driven initiatives in Seville, learn how the zero-waste movement is gaining momentum, encouraging conscious consumer choices and reducing plastic pollution.

Renewable Energy Initiatives:

Explore the renewable energy initiatives that contribute to Spain's commitment to clean energy. From solar farms in Extremadura to wind energy projects in Galicia, this section highlights how the country is harnessing its natural resources to transition towards a more sustainable and eco-friendly energy landscape.

Sustainable Transportation:

Navigate the landscape of sustainable transportation initiatives in Spain. From bike-sharing programs in Barcelona to electric vehicle infrastructure in Bilbao, discover how cities are promoting eco-friendly modes of transportation, reducing carbon emissions, and creating more accessible and sustainable mobility options.

Waste Reduction and Recycling Programs:

Dive into waste reduction and recycling programs that play a crucial role in Spain's eco-friendly practices. From innovative recycling initiatives in Zaragoza to circular economy projects in Malaga, this chapter showcases how communities and businesses are actively working towards minimizing waste and promoting recycling.

Plastic-Free Initiatives:

Explore the plastic-free initiatives that are gaining momentum across Spain. From coastal cleanup campaigns in Valencia to plastic-free market stalls in Granada, learn how individuals and organizations are taking a stand against single-use plastics, contributing to cleaner oceans and a healthier environment.

Sustainable Tourism Practices:

Embark on a journey into sustainable tourism practices that preserve Spain's natural and cultural heritage. From eco-friendly accommodations in the Balearic Islands to responsible tourism initiatives in the Pyrenees, discover how the tourism industry is evolving towards more sustainable and ethical practices.

Case Studies: Inspirational Stories of Eco-Friendly Success:

Delve into case studies that share inspirational stories of eco-friendly success in Spain. Explore how businesses, communities, and individuals are making a positive impact by adopting and promoting sustainable practices. These case studies showcase the diversity and creativity of eco-friendly initiatives across the country.

Conclusion: Nurturing a Sustainable Tomorrow:

As you conclude this exploration of eco-friendly practices in Spain, reflect on the collective efforts to nurture a sustainable tomorrow. May this chapter inspire you to embrace eco-friendly living, make conscious choices, and contribute to the ongoing journey towards a more sustainable, resilient, and harmonious world.

Animal Sanctuaries and Vegan-Friendly Attractions: A Compassionate Tourism Experience

Embark on a journey of compassion as we explore the world of animal sanctuaries and vegan-friendly attractions in Spain. This chapter is a celebration of ethical tourism, offering insights into sanctuaries that provide refuge for animals and attractions that align with the principles of cruelty-free living.

Animal Sanctuaries: Havens of Compassion:

Discover the havens of compassion known as animal sanctuaries, where rescued animals find refuge and care. From farm animal sanctuaries in Catalonia to primate rescue centers in Murcia, this section sheds light on the important work of these sanctuaries, their dedication to animal welfare, and how they provide a transformative experience for visitors.

Vegan-Friendly Wildlife Experiences:

Navigate the realm of vegan-friendly wildlife experiences that prioritize ethical interactions with animals. From eco-conscious whale watching in the Strait of Gibraltar to birdwatching tours in the Ebro Delta, learn how tourism operators are embracing cruelty-free practices, respecting wildlife habitats, and offering enriching experiences for nature enthusiasts.

Vegan-Friendly Attractions: Cultural Exploration with Compassion:

Explore vegan-friendly attractions that merge cultural exploration with compassion. From historical sites in Toledo with vegan dining options to art museums in Bilbao that promote sustainable practices, this section showcases how attractions are adapting to the growing demand for vegan-friendly experiences, offering inclusive and cruelty-free options for visitors.

Interactive Experiences with Rescued Animals:

Delve into interactive experiences that allow visitors to connect with rescued animals in ethical and respectful ways. Whether it's spending a day at a donkey sanctuary in Andalusia or volunteering at a wildlife rehabilitation center in Valencia, learn how these experiences foster a deeper understanding of animal welfare and the importance of compassion.

Educational Programs for Responsible Tourism:

Discover educational programs integrated into responsible tourism initiatives that emphasize the principles of ethical and compassionate travel. From guided tours with wildlife experts to workshops on animal conservation in the Balearic Islands, this chapter explores how tourism can be a force for positive change, raising awareness and encouraging responsible behavior.

Vegan Culinary Experiences at Attractions:

Savor vegan culinary experiences integrated into attractions, creating a harmonious blend of culture, history, and cruelty-free dining. Whether it's exploring ancient castles with plant-based picnics or visiting botanical gardens in Seville with vegan cafe options, learn how attractions are catering to the growing demand for compassionate dining experiences.

Case Studies: Exemplary Models of Compassionate Tourism:

Delve into case studies that spotlight exemplary models of compassionate tourism in Spain. Explore how attractions and sanctuaries are innovatively combining education, wildlife preservation, and vegan-friendly practices to create meaningful and impactful experiences for visitors. These case studies showcase the diversity and success of compassionate tourism initiatives.

Conclusion: Transformative Journeys of Compassion:

As you conclude this exploration of animal sanctuaries and vegan-friendly attractions in Spain, reflect on the transformative journeys of compassion that ethical tourism can offer. May this chapter inspire you to seek out experiences that align with your values, fostering a deeper connection with the natural world and contributing to the well-being of animals and ecosystems alike.

Chapter 9: Traveling as a Vegan: Tips and Tricks

Navigate the diverse culinary landscape of Spain with insights into plant-based dining options. Whether you're exploring the bustling streets of Barcelona or the tranquil towns of Andalusia, this chapter provides tips on finding vegan-friendly restaurants, markets, and hidden gems that celebrate Spain's rich gastronomic heritage.

Equip yourself with the language of veganism to facilitate smooth communication about your dietary preferences. From understanding menu terminology to learning key phrases for dietary inquiries, this section ensures you can navigate

Spanish dining experiences with confidence and ease.

Immerse yourself in the local vegan scene by connecting with communities across Spain. From attending vegan meetups in Madrid to exploring plant-based events in Valencia, learn how to tap into local knowledge, make new friends, and share experiences with like-minded individuals during your travels.

Vegan-Friendly Travel Essentials: A Compassionate Packing Guide

Embark on your travels fully equipped with vegan-friendly essentials that align with your ethical lifestyle. This chapter serves as your compass, guiding you through the process of packing thoughtfully and ensuring a seamless journey while staying true to your plant-based principles.

Vegan-Friendly Luggage and Accessories:

Begin your journey by selecting luggage and accessories that echo your commitment to cruelty-free living. Explore options made from sustainable materials or innovative vegan leather alternatives. This section provides insights into choosing bags, wallets, and travel accessories that align with your ethical choices.

Cruelty-Free Toiletries and Personal Care Products:

Transform your daily self-care routine into an ethical ritual with cruelty-free toiletries and personal care products. From vegan shampoo bars to eco-friendly toothpaste, this chapter guides you in selecting products that prioritize both your well-being and the well-being of our planet.

Portable Plant-Based Snacks and Nourishment:

Satisfy your cravings on the go with a curated selection of portable plant-based snacks. From trail mixes to energy bars and dehydrated fruits, this section provides a variety of travel-friendly snack options that ensure you stay nourished while exploring the diverse landscapes of your destination.

Reusable Containers and Eco-Friendly Utensils:

Optimize your sustainability efforts with reusable containers and eco-friendly utensils. Whether you're enjoying street food or packing your own meals, this chapter offers insights into compact and lightweight options that make it easy to reduce single-use plastic during your travels.

Vegan-Friendly Footwear and Clothing:

Step into your adventures with footwear and clothing that respect animal rights and the environment. From comfortable, stylish vegan shoes to cruelty-free and eco-friendly clothing options, this section helps you curate a travel wardrobe that aligns with your values and the climate of your destination.

Ethical Travel Guides and Resources:

Enhance your travel experience with ethical travel guides and resources. Discover books and online platforms that provide insights into vegan-friendly destinations, sustainable accommodations, and ethical travel practices. This chapter empowers you to plan a trip that not only satisfies your wanderlust but also resonates with your commitment to conscious travel.

Vegan Travel Apps and Language Guides:

Navigate your destination with the help of vegan travel apps and language guides. From locating plant-based eateries to learning essential phrases for dietary inquiries, this section introduces you to digital resources that make your journey more enjoyable, informative, and aligned with your vegan lifestyle.

Sustainable and Vegan-Friendly Travel Gear:

Invest in sustainable and vegan-friendly travel gear that withstands the rigors of exploration. From backpacks made from recycled materials to eco-conscious travel tech, this chapter showcases gear that enhances your travel experience while minimizing your environmental impact.

Vegan Medications and First Aid Supplies:

Prioritize your well-being with vegan medications and first aid supplies. Explore plant-based alternatives to common medications and cruelty-free first aid essentials. This section guides you in creating a travel health kit that aligns with your vegan principles and keeps you prepared for unexpected situations.

Case Studies: Vegan Travel Essentials in Action:

Delve into case studies that illustrate the use of vegan travel essentials in real-world journeys. Learn from the experiences of fellow travelers who have successfully integrated cruelty-free products and sustainable practices into their adventures. These case studies offer practical insights and inspiration for a compassionate and well-prepared travel experience.

Conclusion: Traveling Light, Traveling Right:

As you conclude this chapter on vegan-friendly travel essentials, envision your journeys with a light footprint and a compassionate heart. May these packing tips and ethical choices empower you to explore the world with mindfulness, ensuring that every step you take is in harmony with your values and the well-being of our planet. Safe travels!

Embracing Vegan Spain - A Journey of Compassion

As we draw the curtains on our exploration of "Discovering Vegan Spain," it is a moment to reflect on the vibrant tapestry of experiences, flavors, and compassionate living that define this journey. Spain, a country rich in history, culture, and gastronomy, has proven to be a haven for those embracing a plant-based lifestyle. Our odyssey through its cities, landscapes, and culinary delights has not only been a celebration of veganism but also a testament to the evolving narrative of conscious living in this beautiful nation.

In every chapter, we witnessed the dedication of individuals, communities, and businesses in Spain to weave a more compassionate narrative into the fabric of daily life. From the kitchens of innovative chefs reinventing traditional dishes to the serene landscapes of animal sanctuaries offering solace to rescued creatures, our exploration revealed a Spain that is embracing change, sustainability, and ethical choices.

The journey through Vegan Spain extended beyond culinary escapades. We traversed the intersections of veganism with fashion, beauty, travel, and activism, discovering how the principles of compassion resonate across various aspects of Spanish life. Whether exploring the eco-friendly initiatives transforming urban spaces or connecting with local vegan communities, it became evident that a holistic approach to mindful living is taking root in every corner of the country.

Through the lens of travel, we provided insights into navigating Spain as a vegan, offering practical tips and experiences to make your journeys seamless, enjoyable, and aligned with your ethical choices. The vegan-friendly attractions, sustainable practices, and diverse landscapes beckon travelers to explore Spain with a heart full of compassion and a commitment to leaving a positive impact on the places they visit.

As we conclude this journey, let it serve as an invitation to continue exploring the possibilities of compassionate living, not just in Spain but in every corner of the globe. The stories shared, the flavors savored, and the experiences gained on this odyssey are not just confined to the pages of this book; they are seeds planted for a future where conscious choices, sustainability, and compassion become integral parts of our collective existence.

May "Discovering Vegan Spain" inspire you to embark on your own journeys of exploration, whether it be through the bustling streets of

Madrid, the serene landscapes of Andalusia, or the vibrant festivals of Barcelona. Let it be a compass guiding you towards a life filled with mindful choices, where every step is a dance of compassion, and every meal is a celebration of ethical living.

In closing, I extend my gratitude for joining me on this voyage of discovery. May your path be filled with the joy of conscious living, and may the echoes of compassion resonate in every aspect of your life.

Buen viaje y vive compasivamente – Safe travels, and live compassionately.

Additional book and resources

Books:

"Eating Animals" by Jonathan Safran Foer

A thought-provoking exploration of the ethics and environmental impact of eating animals.

"The China Study" by T. Colin Campbell and Thomas M. Campbell II

An influential book that examines the relationship between diet and health, promoting a plant-based lifestyle.

"Veganomicon" by Isa Chandra Moskowitz and Terry Hope Romero

A comprehensive cookbook offering a diverse range of delicious and accessible vegan recipes.

"How Not to Die" by Michael Greger, M.D.

A guide to evidence-based nutrition, providing insights into preventing and treating chronic diseases through a plant-based diet.

"Animal Liberation" by Peter Singer

A classic in animal rights literature, arguing for the ethical treatment of animals and the adoption of a vegan lifestyle.

Online Resources:

HappyCow (Website and App)

A valuable resource for finding vegan and vegetarian-friendly restaurants and cafes worldwide.

NutritionFacts.org

Run by Dr. Michael Greger, this website provides evidence-based information on nutrition and health, with a focus on plant-based diets.

Vegan Society

A comprehensive resource for information on vegan living, including recipes, guides, and articles.

Plant Based News

An online platform offering news, articles, and videos related to plant-based living, veganism, and ethical choices.

The Vegan Society of Spain (Sociedad Vegana)

Connect with the local vegan community in Spain, access resources, and stay updated on events and initiatives promoting veganism.

These resources can offer a deeper dive into various aspects of veganism, from health and nutrition to ethics and activism. Whether you're looking for delicious recipes, nutritional guidance, or information on animal rights, these books and online platforms can be valuable companions on your journey towards a compassionate and plant-based lifestyle.

About the Author

Greetings, dear reader. I'm Rami Georgiev, an author passionate about unveiling the intricacies of the vegan lifestyle, psychology, and mindfulness. My journey as a writer is fueled by a deep commitment to fostering positive change in both personal and collective spheres.

My exploration of the vegan lifestyle goes beyond dietary choices, delving into the ethical, environmental, and holistic dimensions that define a compassionate and sustainable way of living. In each page, I aim to offer insights that not only nourish the body but also resonate with a broader understanding of our interconnectedness with the world.

In the realm of psychology, I navigate the complex terrain of the human mind with a profound understanding of its intricacies. My work invites readers to embark on a journey of self-discovery, unlocking the potential for growth and transformation within. With empathy as my guide, I strive to provide practical insights that empower individuals to navigate the complexities of the modern world with grace and resilience.

Mindfulness, for me, is not just a practice but a way of life. Through a blend of contemplative traditions, stress reduction techniques, and the art of mindful living, I aim to make ancient wisdom accessible to the contemporary reader. My goal is to offer practical tools that help cultivate awareness and navigate the challenges of daily life with mindful intention.

With a background spanning various fields, I bring a multidimensional perspective to my writing. Whether unraveling the mysteries of the mind or guiding readers on a journey toward a more conscious existence, I strive to create a space for reflection, growth, and positive change.

As you explore my books, consider this an invitation to challenge assumptions, cultivate awareness, and embrace a lifestyle that reflects not only personal well-being but also a profound connection to the world we inhabit. Thank you for joining me on this journey of exploration, introspection, and mindful living.

Warm regards,

Rami Georgiev